HATIKVAH HOLOCAUST
EDUCATION & RESOURCE CENTER
1160 DICKINSON STREET
SPRINGFIELD, MA 01108

Ziemian, Joseph   B / o

THE CIGARETTE SELLERS OF THREE CROSSES SQUARE

DATE DUE			

TEMPLE BETH EL LIBRARY
SPRINGFIELD, MASSACHUSETTS

The Cigarette Sellers

OF THREE CROSSES SQUARE

The Cigarette Sellers

OF THREE CROSSES SQUARE

by JOSEPH ZIEMIAN

Translated from the Polish
by JANINA DAVID

LERNER PUBLICATIONS COMPANY
Minneapolis

Z940.43
Zie

1975 Edition

New material and epilogue copyright © 1975 by Lerner Publications Company.
Original text copyright © 1970 by Joseph Zeimian.

ALL RIGHTS RESERVED

No part of this book may be reproduced in any form whatsoever without
permission in writing from the publisher except for the inclusion of
brief quotations in an acknowledged review.

First published in the United States 1975 by Lerner Publications
Company, 241 First Avenue North, Minneapolis, Minnesota 55401.
Published simultaneously in Canada by J. M. Dent & Sons (Canada) Ltd.

Manufactured in the United States of America

International Standard Book Number: 0-8225-0757-9
Library of Congress Catalog Card Number: 54-11900

CONTENTS

Foreword

THE JEWISH COMMUNITY in Warsaw had existed for almost seven centuries. At first the main occupations of its members were commerce and crafts, but with time they infiltrated other professions, contributing notably to the sciences, culture and art in Poland.

In 1939 there were almost 400,000 Jews in Warsaw; today there are about 5,000. This was the largest Jewish community in Europe. Its members lived mainly in the northern district of the town, around Nalewki, Gesia, Franciszkanska, Zamenhoff, Smocza and Muranowska streets. The community ran its own schools; its full cultural life (in Polish, Yiddish and Hebrew) included a flourishing literature, philosophy and arts and a fast-developing press.

The Jewish Council—an autonomous organisation—looked after the welfare of every member of the community, from his birth to the allotment of his burial place. There were two Jewish hospitals, a social service department, religious institutions and political and youth organisations. The Jews had their representatives in the Sejm and Senat whose main task was to combat increasing antisemitism and restrictions of freedom and civil rights imposed on the Jewish minority.

Conditions worsened perceptibly in the 1930s, under the

7

influence of their German neighbour. Then came the war: the early period of unrest, Poles and Jews fighting together on the Warsaw barricades and, finally, the tragic days of the occupation.

The persecution of Jews grew worse daily, from the cutting of old men's beards, the plundering and burning of shops, deportations for forced labour, to the establishment of the ghetto (November 1940). The whole Jewish community was concentrated in a small district, with several families crowded into a flat. The area was surrounded by high walls and barbed wire, isolating it from the rest of the town and from the Polish inhabitants. Warsaw was split into two sections: the Jewish and the Polish or Aryan one.

Soon the death penalty was introduced for crossing the ghetto walls. Inside the ghetto opportunities for earning a living fell to a minimum. Under the system of enforced pauperisation, the face of the ghetto changed rapidly, while terror and slave labour for the 'new masters of the world' reduced morale. Hunger increased from day to day. The official rations were less than sufficient and food smuggled from the Aryan side very expensive.

The special treatment devised by the Germans—they cut off the water supply, stopped refuse collection, etc.—brought on an epidemic of typhus. Hundreds died daily from hunger and disease. The situation deteriorated considerably when the German authorities resettled thousands of destitute Jews from the neighbouring towns and villages in the ghetto.

But the people had to live and eat somehow, and it was then that the children's army of little smugglers set out for the Aryan side. Stealing across the walls and barbed wire, they emerged into the Polish streets and from there smuggled food to the starving ghetto. Some of them begged for a bowl of soup, a crust of bread or a few *groszy* with which they could buy food for the rest of their families. Many of the children were hunted and shot by the Germans and fell under the ghetto walls. Their places were taken by others, since this was the only way to keep their families alive.

For the majority of the little heroes, the fight for survival was ended by the first resettlement action of July 1942. Almost all of them were sent to the extermination camps. A small group remained on the Aryan side unable to return home; these learned only gradually of the tragic fate of their families.

Among the children there were some who carried arms as well as food for the ghetto. They had been recruited into the ranks of the organised resistance fighters and served as liaison with the non-Jewish side. Most of them fell later, in the resettlement actions or in the ghetto uprising of 1943. Only a small group survived—and it is with their struggles and adventures that this story is concerned.

Introduction

THE WAR HAD ended. I was left alone, conscious of a great emptiness around me. My family had perished. Nothing was left, not even the graves to weep on.

All that remained of my past were the notes and commentaries on my work in the Jewish Resistance Movement during the occupation. They survived by a miracle, hidden during the Warsaw Uprising of 1944. I did not think, when hiding them, that I should ever find them again or that they would be of any use. But when I brought them out from their subterranean hiding-place, page after yellowed page, barely legible, they suddenly became a hidden treasure. I began to read them again. And in them I found details of an organised group of Jewish children: the cigarette sellers from the Three Crosses Square. The excerpts I read of our conversations, and the photographs I had taken, revived in my memory one of the most curious and moving episodes of the occupation: the story of these children.

After their escape from the ghetto they led an adventurous and independent existence on the Aryan side of Warsaw. Sentenced to death, hounded and harried at every step, they found a way of surviving in the jungle of the occupation. They knew how to defend themselves and how to fight for their existence; they knew—unlike so many adults—how to help each other.

Growing in number, they lived at first by begging, by singing in the streets or by casual labour, and later by selling cigarettes on the Three Crosses Square. They were very brave. Some of them used to smuggle food and arms to the ghetto and took part in the uprisings of 1943 and 1944. These were the luckiest; of more than 20 children, the majority have survived.

From their stories I have chosen only those fragments which concern the group as a whole. But a whole book could be written about each one of them.

The Meeting

AUTUMN 1943

THE LAST SHOTS of the fighting in the ghetto had ceased long ago. Only the burnt-out shells of houses and the walls surrounding this cemetery of nearly half a million Jews remained. Warsaw was *Judenrein*. The streets had returned to their normal way of life under the occupation, and the fantastic stories about Jewish fighters were becoming rare. The passers-by were no longer seeing a refugee from the ghetto in every other person. One could again travel to Zoliborz via Bonifraterska Street (during the fighting in the ghetto there was a compulsory diversion via Zakroczymska Street). Only the German posters decreeing the death penalty for harbouring Jews bore witness to the continuing existence of Jewish survivors.

Very few Jews had managed to escape extinction, often by most complicated methods. Having arrived at the Aryan side, they now led a more or less camouflaged existence. They hid in cellars and in ruins; a certain number were hidden by Poles, in some cases through friendship, in others by paying. Every day was a lottery with survival at any price at stake. But time was not on their side. Days, hours even, dragged with incredible slowness. Sometimes it seemed that 'the days of wrath' would last for ever. Only in the depths of one's soul a little spark of hope remained. The nearer death came, the harder one fought for life.

The autumn of 1943 was my first in hiding. I had a false *Kennkarta* (identity card issued by the Germans), a false *Ausweis* (certificate of employment) and a fabricated life history. Such a history, well thought out and memorised, was an indispensable condition of survival. Even when awakened from the deepest sleep, I could immediately trot out my 'employment' and my 'father's' name without a single mistake. Not to have a family was suspect. It didn't do any harm, either, to suggest that one had contacts with the Polish Resistance. The underground organisations enjoyed great respect among Poles.

I was a member of the Resistance Movement, in fact, but with only the Jewish one. This, however, I could never admit. The double deception—regarding my origins and contacts with the Resistance—involved double precautions. Every step had to be calculated, every word thought out and every new contact summed up immediately. A facial expression, a gesture, a detail of dress dictated the degree of care one had to take.

There were various means of avoiding undesirable meetings in the streets. Sometimes, in order to avoid someone's eyes, one had to blow one's nose, pretend to tie a shoelace or study a shop window. In the window-pane one could also unobtrusively observe the passers-by. This was a great school of human psychology. However circumspect a man might be, if he lost his self-confidence for a fraction of a second, he was done for. In this ocean of hostility any false move could prove fatal.

One October day I was going down Nowy Swiat towards Jerozolimskie Avenue. On the first floor, at No. 23, there was an R.G.O.* soup kitchen. I used to eat my dinners there almost daily. It was getting late and I was in a hurry to arrive before the place closed. The street was crowded. Suddenly I noticed two boys, one about 16, the other perhaps 13. The face of the elder boy seemed vaguely familiar from ghetto days. Jewish children? Is it possible, I wondered? No, I must be wrong. Several months had passed since the complete destruction of the ghetto. Nearly every day Jews found on the Aryan

* R.G.O.—*Rada Glowna Opiekuncza*—Official Polish Social Welfare Department.

13

side were being executed. To live in the occupation jungle demanded unusual energy, powers of invention and other qualities. Many an adult broke down under the strain of the daily battle; how then could children . . .?

Suddenly our eyes met and that was enough. I had no more doubts. It seems there is some truth in the saying that 'Jews can smell each other at a distance'. I decided to establish contact with the boys, but had to proceed with great care, without disclosing my identity or plans. To approach a stranger and gain his confidence was no mean feat. Anyway, the fear was mutual. Chance meetings between Jews, even among acquaintances, unless they were true friends, usually ended with the words: "Excuse me, I don't know you, you must be mistaken," and a fast retreat in the opposite direction. Every Jew was afraid of his own shadow.

The street urchins, whose only possessions were their meagre clothing, did not attract any special attention from the *shmalzers* (blackmailers who denounced Jews to the Germans) and were therefore in less danger than the adults. Nevertheless, they too had to be extremely careful, and anyone trying to approach them had to observe 'the rules of the game', taking care not to 'blow' their cover.

Entering the house, I turned my head and our eyes met again. The ice was broken. Probably the boys craved contact with a kindred soul. They followed me inside and when I sat down at a table they took the next one. The customers were mainly beggars, refugees from the districts incorporated into the Reich, redundant civil servants and impoverished intellectuals. Many of the Jews living in hiding also visited the kitchens, which functioned in various parts of the town. The most popular subject of conversation was the war.

I felt slightly safer amidst all the poverty which surrounded me. I looked at the boys. The elder of the two had a round face, wise blue eyes and thick, wavy, dark-blond hair. In a word, he looked Aryan. He seemed energetic and sure of himself. His clothes were not too bad; a clean white shirt and a fairly decent suit. The younger boy looked more Semitic: a narrow face, rather a long nose, dark-blue eyes, gentle and gay. His hair fell around his temples. He wore a longish jacket and ragged trousers and his bare feet were blue with cold. The boys looked around the room and I felt their eyes on me. I sensed that they wanted to approach me. I finished my meal quickly and left, imperceptibly beckoning them to follow. In the courtyard the elder boy began: "Excuse me, but didn't you work in Placowka at the *Ostbahn?"*

"Did you?" I asked in return.

He nodded, though this was equivalent to admitting his identity, since Placowka was a work place, outside the ghetto, for Jews only.

"What are you doing here? Where do you live?" he asked avidly. In all probability my not answering his first question had reassured him as to my own origins. I found myself in an awkward situation. I could not reveal my occupation or address. This was the basic principle of the clandestine existence I was leading.

"I live in the ruins in town . . . I manage." I wanted to show that my own life was similar to theirs. It helped to gain their confidence and at the same time reduced the possibility of blackmail or denunciation on their part.

"If you want, you can sleep with us at a Polish woman's place," offered the elder boy. I was dumbfounded. A voluntary offer of a 'den' was in those times an extremely rare phenomenon.

"And you? What do you do? Aren't you afraid of being together?" I asked.

"We work at the Three Crosses Square. There are many more of us. We stick together and we're doing all right," said the younger boy.

"The Polish boys sometimes try to pick on us, demanding to see our documents, but we can handle them," added the elder.

I couldn't believe my ears. It seemed like a figment of the

* *Deutsch Ostbahn*—German railway network in the occupied territories of Eastern Europe.

imagination. No one would have believed it then. We talked for a while and, finding some excuse to avoid their offer of help, I made an arrangement to meet them at the same place the following day.

Next day, I arrived at the appointed place together with one of my 'charges', a Jew in hiding who was being helped by our underground organisation and whom I had informed of my meeting with the boys. I did not yet have a clear view of the situation, not knowing what the boys might be planning. During the meeting, the other man was to stay in the vicinity of a German radio loudspeaker (a 'barker') at the corner of Nowy Swiat and Jerozolimskie Avenue, keeping a watch over the entrance to No. 23. It was an indispensable precaution in the circumstances. In case of danger he would warn me with a whistle.

At the appointed time the elder boy arrived at the house, walked across the courtyard and approached a side staircase.

"Who's the 'character' who talked to you in the street?" were his first words. I realised I had been watched. "Was he a shmalzer?" he inquired suspiciously.

"No, he asked for directions," I answered nonchalantly and to change the subject asked, "Where is your friend?"

"He's coming. He's on the first floor, at the observation post," replied the boy calmly. "You know, sometimes you can bring on the shmalzers without meaning to. They like following people."

This astonishing confidence dispelled my last doubts. It revealed also that the boys were careful and knew the rules. In a little while we were joined by the younger boy.

"How are you? Where do you sleep? How do you live? Did any of your family escape from the ghetto?" Both boys showered me with questions. I answered some, while others obviously had to be avoided.

"Unfortunately, none of my family escaped."

"We are also alone," they confessed. The boys made me feel a fellow soul. Nothing brings people together more than a common fate.

"Bull, someone's coming!" whispered the younger boy.

Footsteps sounded clearly on the stairs. Whose? We held our breath and listened. The steps drew nearer, a door creaked, then slammed loudly. Someone had entered the ground floor flat. Silence fell again. The danger had passed.

"What do you mean, 'Bull'?" I asked the elder boy.

"They call me Bull at the Three Crosses Square. Almost everyone has a nickname. He's called Conky. See what a long nose he's got?" We both laughed. The younger boy looked hurt.

"He takes everything so seriously," explained Bull.

"Are there many of you at the Square?" I asked Conky, to draw him out a little.

"Over a dozen. We sell cigarettes, we stick together and we're tough," was the quick reply.

"Business is booming. Come with us and see for yourself," added Bull. From under the thick thatch of hair his eyes shone with gaiety and confidence. The offer was tempting. Frankly, I did not really think it possible then that such a group of Jewish children could exist in the very heart of the German district of Warsaw. I decided to go with them to the Three Crosses Square.

We left, Bull leading, Conky and I following each other at a distance so as not to attract attention.

Crowds had gathered round the 'barker' where the news was being broadcast. We stopped a moment. They were expecting news about the withdrawal of the Germans, and held their breath as they listened to every word. "Evacuation is being prepared." One young man shook his friend. A glance and a tiny smile sufficed for a reply. "After a short battle contact was broken off with the enemy." The listeners exchanged looks. A smothered whisper of gibes was heard. We continued to walk.

At 5 Nowy Swiat we passed the Four Seasons restaurant, a place *Nur für Deutsche* ('For Germans only'). Through the open door we heard the gay voices of German soldiers. Here, Bull informed me, was Conky's business place.

A moment later we were at the Three Crosses Square.

A map of Three Crosses Square and its environs

1. R.G.O. soup kitchen
2. The restaurant, Vier Jahreszeiten
3. Julius Meinl shop
4. The church of St. Aleksander
5. The tram conductors' shelter
6. The Deaf, Dumb, and Blind Institute
7. The photographer's stand
8. The Apollo cinema
9. Soldatenheim
10. The transit point of the Hungarian soldiers
11. The S.S. barracks
12. The post of German gendarmerie
13. The News theatre
14. Julius Meinl shop
15. Grandma's house
16. R.G.O. soup kitchen

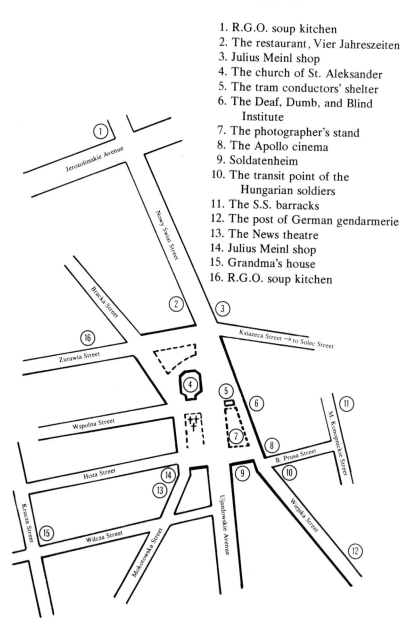

Three Crosses Square of pre-war Warsaw

Five of the cigarette sellers: left to right, Toothy and Zbyszek (back row); Frenchy, Burek (the Peasant), and Conky (front row)

Three Crosses Square

THE SQUARE RESOUNDED with the voices of tramdrivers gathered at the terminus, the cries of newspaper boys and the patter of cigarette sellers trying to attract customers. The gabble of German soldiers reminded one that the town was still occupied. Tram No. 0—*Nur für Deutsche*—crossed the Square in the direction of Ujazdowskie Avenue. The Three Crosses Square, which before the war was one of the busiest places in the centre of Warsaw, now lay in the heart of the German district. There was a German gendarmerie at the nearby Wiejska Street; the Y.M.C.A. building on Konopnicka Street was now a barracks for German SS-men; the grocery shop 'Julius Meinl' on the corner of Hoza Street was also for Germans only. Another such shop was situated diagonally opposite, at the corner of Ksiazeca Street. The Polish inhabitants preferred to avoid the Square. Only the Church of St. Aleksander in the middle of it remained as an unchanged landmark from before the war.

As we arrived a detachment of SS was marching through the Square. Hobnailed boots stamped on the pavement and loud singing reverberated against the walls of the surrounding buildings. From the former Queen Jadwiga High School, now a German soldiers' home, came sounds of music. Boys holding cigarettes rushed to and fro outside the building. Two of them were so absorbed in a quarrel that they did not notice us at all. But a sharp whistle from Conky stopped the row at once. They gathered round us, eyeing me with suspicion. Bull, who was acting as my guide, signalled to them and they turned away as if they didn't know him.

"They are ours, from Saska Kepa," whispered Bull. I studied them carefully. One of the boys, Jankiel, looked about 10 years old (in fact he was 13). He had an oval face, laughing eyes and both his nose and the peak of his dirty cyclist's cap turned up cheekily. His buck teeth explained his nickname, Toothy. He was poorly dressed, his thin bare legs and feet showing through torn trousers which hung below his knees. His companion, Zbyszek, who looked about 15, seemed typically Aryan, and had sharp eyes. The same could be said for his tongue which was coarse enough to shatter my ears from a distance. He looked like a tramp; the open shirt revealed a pimply body, and a broken-down pair of wooden clogs completed his rather unsavoury appearance. I admit I could not quite believe in his Jewish origin. However, I had neither time nor opportunity to ask questions. In a twinkling the whole group had surrounded an approaching German soldier. Each wanted to sell his cigarettes or to exchange them for tinned food or sardines.

Further down, in the garden of the Square, other soldiers were having their photos taken against a landscape painted on canvas—*Gruss aus Warschau*. The Polish photographer had his hands full at that moment. But when there were no Germans, the cigarette boys took their place, posing in front of the camera.

The old Totalisator building at the corner of the Square and Prus Street was now a transit camp for Hungarian soldiers collaborating with the Germans. The entrance to the building was guarded by a stone lion. Next to it stood a 14-year-old boy, a box of cigarettes in one hand, the other hand on the lion's head. Noticing Bull he smiled conspiratorially. His features showed clearly that he, too, was Jewish.

"That one is 'Frenchy', from Paris," said Bull. "His parents were resettled in Warsaw because of their Polish nationality. We were together in a transport from the ghetto; some time later I met him in Praga [a suburb of Warsaw east of the Vistula]. As yet he is 'dizzy'—he hasn't entered into the swim of things."

A few boys circulated among the Hungarians. Using sign language they somehow managed to understand each other and business was booming. Bull pointed out another boy, Pawel, a friend of Zbyszek and Toothy, who also seemed about 15. Under a ski cap pulled down to his eyes his face looked thin and peaky; his clothes too were torn and dirty. But for Bull's information I could have passed him many times without suspecting his origin.

The cigarette boys pushed and jostled and Pawel behaved exactly like the others, never giving way. To retreat could arouse suspicion.

We were ready to go to the nearby Y.M.C.A. building on Konopnicka Street. Here, as was explained to me later, stood the pitch of a 12-year-old Jewish boy, who had been nicknamed 'Burek' (the Peasant). I lost sight of Bull and found him again among the Hungarians. He, too, had to see about his daily bread: I saw him doing some quick business. After a few minutes we returned to the Square. The Napoleon cinema, renamed Apollo by the Germans, was also *Nur für Deutsche*. There we found another Jewish boy. He was nine years old, thin and bedraggled. Despite his blue eyes and blond hair I had no doubts as to his origin. The Semitic nose, and even more his frightened eyes, spoke for themselves. He stood against a wall with packets of cigarettes under one arm, trying not to attract attention. 'Little Stasiek' was not selling anything but helped the others by carrying their supplies. He was their walking storehouse.

Bull told me some important things about him. His parents had been rich. In order to save him they handed him over to Polish acquaintances. The parents were killed in the ghetto and the boy wandered from Pole to Pole without being able to remain in any one place for any length of time because of his appearance. In the end he came by chance to Three Crosses Square, and the Jewish cigarette sellers took him under their protection.

"We've been having trouble with him since the beginning, commented Bull. "The Polish boys working at the Square pick on him and rob him and then the bigger ones among us have to fight to get our stores back."

In front of the iron railings at the entrance to the Blind, Deaf and Dumb Institute, two cigarette sellers were quarrelling loudly. The girl, Teresa, wore a torn dress and a dirty sweater. Fair hair fell to her shoulders. There was a big scar on her forehead above one eye. The boy, Yosek, looked Jewish. Dark eyes and curly black hair were dangerously indicative of his origin. His clothes were torn; he looked tired and he limped, which explained his nickname, Hoppy.

These were the founders of the gang, comrades in heart and soul.

"That was my client!" cried Teresa.

"No, he was mine!" maintained Hoppy.

Bull separated them with a few quiet words.

"Is she also one of us?" I asked.

"Yes, she is."

"And these two?" I inquired, pointing out two boys running across the Square with cigarette packets.

"The one without shoes is; his name is Zenek, he is Pawel's brother. The other one is Polish."

I looked, unable to believe my eyes. The fantastic tale told me by Bull and Conky only the day before, about this group of children selling cigarettes at the Three Crosses Square, was only a pale reflection of reality. What I saw surpassed my wildest dreams.

"This is not all, there are others, in other places," added Bull triumphantly.

When Bull left to attend to his business, I decided to walk across the Square once more and have a closer look at these children. In the garden, in the middle of the Square a few boys were quarrelling furiously. The leader was a boy of about

14 whom I recognised. It was the same Zenek I had seen before. Zenek had an oval face, dark, penetrating eyes and dark hair falling over his forehead. He was dressed in a filthy colourless shirt, with knee-length trousers, like a grubby urchin. He looked at me sharply when I spoke to him, and three other boys walking nearby surrounded me quickly, curious and obviously anxious.

"Have you been working here long?" I asked.

"Look at the time," exclaimed one of the group, pointing to the clock of the Institute. "We should be at Saska Kepa!" I realised they were afraid to talk to me.

I left the Three Crosses Square shortly afterwards, profoundly impressed by my discovery. The following day I returned. It was early. There were the same ragged little figures, the same voices. the newspaper boys and the cigarette sellers.

Two boys—Zenek and Toothy—barred the way of a passer-by.

"Sir, Egyptian cigarettes. How much, how much sir? These are originals. The lot for only thirty zlotys," Zenek praised his merchandise.

"Too expensive, he sells them for only twenty-five," the client pointed across to Toothy.

"Twenty-five? Sir, those are 'substitutes', not worth even twenty."

I listened to this discussion from the side. The boys bargained and traded with all their might. I crossed over towards the Deaf and Dumb Institute. Teresa stood leaning against the railings while Hoppy hovered nearby.

"What have you got?" asked one man.

"Home-made, Sea-gulls, Egyptians, all kinds," the girl hurried to reply.

The client examined one of the packets.

"These are substitutes. Have you got any good ones?" he asked in a lowered voice.

"The cheap ones are substitutes. Perhaps this sort?" she suggested.

The client picked the packet up carefully and smelt the cigarettes.

"Hm. You see. These are Government ones, I understand these things." He put them in his pocket and asked the price.

"Thirty."

"Why so expensive?"

"Cheaper, it's impossible. Do you want good merchandise? That's the price."

The client took the money out of his wallet, handed it to Teresa and went away. The girl breathed on it in her palm for luck and put it in her pocket. Hoppy winked at her with satisfaction. "A fool will believe anything," joked the girl. "He'll pay if he hasn't any sense. Pity I didn't ask thirty-five—*they* do!" She pointed in the direction of the Polish boys.

"You'd better watch out," he warned her.

I listened to this discussion, and then in order to get closer to them, also bought some cigarettes.

"Aren't you cold without overcoats?" I asked innocently.

"Cold? We're too hot," answered Hoppy, and they exchanged meaningful glances.

"And how old are you?" I asked the boy.

He gave me a sidelong glance, and then looked both ways. Clearly my question was suspect.

The voice of the girl interrupted: "What's that to you?" she said sharply, and that was the end of that. I was saved from an embarrassing situation by Bull's arrival.

"They don't want to talk to you, eh?" he asked with an ironic smile, and turned to Hoppy:

"Don't worry, he's one of ours."

Immediately the ice dissolved between us. We chatted for a bit. Suddenly Conky arrived, out of breath from running.

"Look, he's come back to the Square," Conky shouted, pointing at a small child who had arrived on the scene. It was Bolus, the favourite of the gang of cigarette sellers. Bolus was seven years old. He was dressed in a woman's ragged fur coat, which was tied with cord. A torn shirt showed underneath. His trousers, which were torn and fastened at one side

23

with a safety pin, were too big for him and dragged along the ground. On his feet were broken wooden clogs from which his bare toes peeped out. Under his filthy beret was a mass of dark uncombed hair. He had a pleasant face and intelligent eyes, now looking fearfully at his surroundings.

When Bull noticed him, he turned to go over to him. But two Polish boys about 12 to 14 years old rushed in front of the boy and barred the way.

"Yid, give us money!" shouted one, and the other gripped him. The small child began to retreat. Then Bull intervened. He pushed one Polish boy with all his force, and threatened the other.

"Uncle of the Jews! Shield of a Jew, bet you're a Jew-boy too!" shouted the two Polish boys as they ran away. This really worried Bull.

"Hey, get moving," he shouted to Bolus, "I don't want to see you here anymore! We'll meet tonight at 'Granny's'." The little boy burst into tears.

Hoppy, who noticed my surprise, explained that the presence of Bolus endangered both the child himself and the bigger boys, because rumours were going round the Square that he was a Jew.

The attacks on Bolus made me aware of the danger that lay in wait for the cigarette sellers, and I decided to strengthen my relations with them and to help them as much as I could. I made myself a permanent guest in the Square and slowly became acquainted with all the boys. With a great deal of effort I succeeded in getting out of them details of their movements.

In the beginning they were suspicious and talked unwillingly, and every attempt to note down their stories met strong opposition on their part. My appearance in the Square and my daily visits there caused quite a storm. I was later told that on one of the first days there I was the subject of a heated discussion in the loft at Granny's, the old woman in Krucza Street who gave them refuge. Since I was not their age I could not myself enter into their secrets. I had appeared from nowhere, not wanting their help—a kind of 'Nosy Parker' who tortured them with questions.

"This new man, he is some kind of suspicious type," remarked Teresa.

"Why does he go from one to the other, asking questions about the past? What does all this matter to him?" Zenek asked, expressing the general doubt.

Fortunately I had gained the trust of Bull, whose authority was great. His decisive word was: "Don't be afraid, he's one of ours. I have a sense of smell." This was enough to reduce their fear, especially when Conky agreed with Bull.

From then on they received me with open friendliness in the Square.

This group of Jewish children, wandering around under the very noses of a thousand policemen, gendarmes, Gestapo men and ordinary spies, constituted an unexplained and inexplicable phenomenon, no less mysterious for being real.

A Helping Hand

ONE EVENING, a few days later, in the secret room at 58, 6th of August Street (now Nowowiejska Street), a meeting took place of the Jewish National Committee.

We sat around a large table, set—to avoid suspicion—with cups of coffee and a plate of biscuits. Those present were: 'Michael' (Dr. Adolf Berman), 'Basia' (Barbara Temkin-Bermanowa), 'Bogusia' (Klima Fuswerk-Krymko), 'Czeslawa' (Lotta Wegmeister), 'Stasia' (Helena Merenholc), 'Wanda' (Bela Elster-Rotenberg), and myself ('Jozio'). We spoke in low voices; now and again someone would get up, go to the window and look at the street through drawn curtains.

After a short introduction by Michael, those present gave accounts of their recent activities, especially in the field of material aid. Next came details of future plans and the allocation of funds for continuing help. The money was distributed to Jews in hiding through special Jewish and Polish liaison officers, each of whom had a certain number of charges to look after.

In principle, every Jew in hiding and known to the Committee received 500 zlotys per month. This was sufficient for a modest existence. In some cases the sum was increased, as when a person was forced to pay an exorbitant price for his accommodation or was being blackmailed. Those of particular value to the community—scientists, intellectuals, artists, former public personalities, and escaped fighters from the ghetto—also received a higher rate.

Often the allocation of funds led to sharp arguments. Every member present was responsible for his charges. The majority of those cared for by Stasia, Bogusia and Czeslawa were intellectuals and included many names well-known in Warsaw. Basia, who was Michael's right hand, and Wanda had under their care many public figures. There were few well-known names among the 300-odd in my care. The majority were artisans and young intellectual workers or just people whom I had met by chance and identified as Jews. Most of them had no permanent safe den; after their escape from the ghetto they had hidden on the Aryan side in ruins, cellars and open fields. They, in particular, needed special attention and help.

When the current matters were settled I informed the meeting of my discovery: the cigarette sellers of Three Crosses Square. Although we had some children among our charges, all of them were hidden with a member of their own family or with friends of their parents. Now, however, we had found children alone, existing without anyone's help.

The plan to establish closer contact with these children needed careful examination. We had to decide on the appropriate tactics and on the best form of care. Two separate plans emerged during the ensuing discussion. Some of us felt that the children should be taken away from the Square and placed, two or three together, in so-called 'dens', which were not easy to find. Others maintained that, although the Jewish Underground could strengthen their spirits and give them courage, we had to proceed with great care, slowly gaining the group's confidence and friendship, but without telling them anything about the existence of our organisation—otherwise we might bring disaster both to them and to ourselves.

In the end the second consideration prevailed. We decided to leave the children where they had been found, in the life they were used to. Their appearance, behaviour and occupation camouflaged their Jewish origin quite successfully. Only the

27

Polish boys with whom they were working could, after long observation, become suspicious about any of them. In that event, the child or children concerned would have to be isolated from the rest and hidden in a Polish house.

All present agreed that the boys needed false documents, without of course letting them know of the existence of a whole 'factory' set up for their manufacture. It was also agreed to help them financially and to provide them with clothes. But even here danger lurked. A sudden change in their behaviour or appearance could arouse the suspicions of the others. We had to proceed with care. I decided to take them on as my personal charges and my offer met with the full agreement of the other members.

The following morning I went to my 'office', a little greengrocer's at 5 Sedziowska Street. The owner of the shop, Mrs. Ewa Brzoska, or 'Grandma' as she was known to all her customers, was a vigorous, pink-cheeked woman of about 65, lively and good-humoured, with a heart wide open to all human woes. She helped Jews, knowing full well that they were Jews, by all means at her disposal. She fed children, hid the escapees from the nearby German workshop, the *Heereskraftfahrpark;* stored Jewish Underground literature, false documents, printing machinery, blank forms for birth certificates, and a great deal of other dangerously compromising material. Grandma's shop was an important link in the Jewish Underground, serving both as a meeting-place and a letter-box. Here I sometimes met my 'clients'.

The news about the children filled Grandma with such joy, one would think she had found at least a first cousin. She wanted to know all the details and offered once more to help. Having dealt with the current business at 'the office' I went to my rendezvous with Bull. He was already waiting. Conky was hovering nearby. In a few minutes we were sitting together on the staircase of an adjacent house.

"Just imagine," I said. "I have been able to establish contact with a Polish woman working for the Resistance. Through her I might be able to get you some papers."

Bull jumped for joy. The possession of 'Aryan' papers surpassed his wildest dreams. Only very few among the boys had birth certificates, the others managing without—which increased the danger a hundredfold in case of an inspection.

"In the meantime, here is 500 zlotys for cigarettes," I added, taking the money out of my pocket.

But the boys refused to accept it. At first I thought it was too little.

"Take it, I'll try to get you some more tomorrow," I tried again.

"No, we don't need money," maintained Bull. I was surprised.

"If someone really wants to help us, then let him take young Bolus away. Almost everyone at the Square knows he is Jewish. We can all get caught because of him," explained Bull, while Conky nodded in agreement.

I promised I would take their case to the 'Polish woman from the Resistance'. (There could be no question of divulging my own membership.) We said good-bye and I left. Not far from the house I saw Hoppy. And suddenly a picture of hundreds and thousands of children, begging and loitering in the ghetto, sprang to my mind. While the ghetto existed, these were the children who had supported their families by begging and smuggling. When the ghetto was liquidated, only a few managed to escape. Hoppy was one of them.

Little Smugglers

BEFORE THE WAR Hoppy's parents were fairly prosperous. His father earned a good living and his mother was able to stay at home to look after the house. The six children were all at school or kindergarten. The house was clean and comfortable. Every Friday, the traditional fish graced their table.

When the Germans entered Warsaw and the ghetto was closed, the family's circumstances changed almost overnight. Their shop, the only source of income, was lost; poverty entered their lives and soon there was nothing to eat.

"Mummy, I'll go to the other side and bring something," offered 12-year-old Hoppy.

"No, as long as my eyes can see I won't let a child of mine go begging. I'd rather starve to death!"

Hoppy's mother had a sewing machine and could sew a little. She found work among Poles who had a pass to enter the ghetto. They paid with a loaf of bread or a few kilos of potatoes. His father sold his personal belongings and bought some fat or horse meat with the money. Soon, however, there was nothing left to sell, and the days of real hunger began.

"Mummy, I'll go to the other side, I'll bring some bread," begged Hoppy.

"No, I won't let you, you may get killed."

Misery pervaded everything. The flat was empty and cold. The children wandered listlessly around the courtyard. Hoppy's six-year-old sister cried day and night with hunger.

"It won't be long now, soon the war will be over," repeated their father over and over like an old song. But he, too, was growing weaker. His cheek bones seemed sharper and more prominent, his arms and legs were losing their strength.

When Hoppy again asked permission to go to the other side, no one answered. He was wise enough to understand this silence, and asked his father for ten zlotys. Next morning he left the house. Despite the early hour, the streets were full of people hurrying to work inside the ghetto or to the German workshops outside.

Hoppy's brown eyes, coal-black hair, bare feet blue with cold, torn overcoat with special, deep inside pockets for smuggling potatoes, left no doubt as to his origins. Against these overwhelming odds he had only his sharp wits and the unshakable desire to save his starving family.

First of all he had to get out. The work parties leaving the ghetto waited in a queue for inspection at the sentry post, at the corner of Leszno and Zelazna streets. Hoppy manoeuvring skilfully between the men, managed to leave with them. With the money his father had given him, he bought two loaves of bread in the first shop he found open. He returned to the ghetto in the same way he had left. But he had crossed the 'frontier', and as soon as he was inside outstretched eager hands with money reached for his bread. Hoppy sold one loaf for 14 zlotys and with the other ran home as fast as he could. He returned the ten zlotys to his father and put the second loaf on the table. His mother burst into tears and kissed him.

On the following day Hoppy went out again for bread from the Aryan side. After a few days he began bringing home a rucksack full of potatoes, and armfuls of bread, just as many other children were doing.

It became a regular excursion. Usually he left by the guard post, although sometimes he would infiltrate through the wall. On the Aryan side shmalzers would sometimes take his money from him by force. On several occasions they took his food. After some days he learned to negotiate with them and to deliver himself from their hands.

"My darling son! Our saviour!" cried his mother each day. His little sisters were playing in the courtyard again. For the first time in many months mother scrubbed the neglected floors. At dinner, their only hot meal, Hoppy sat in the place of honour, the armchair, at the head of the table.

One day in the winter of 1941–42, Hoppy returned home laden with potatoes, but with a burning face and eyes shining with fever. He was shaking with cold. It was typhus. The saviour of his family found himself in hospital. Two days later his mother and sister also fell ill and a week later Hoppy's mother died. He and his sister survived and staggered towards home. There they found their father and an elder brother, Meir, lying on the floor. During Hoppy's illness they had almost nothing to eat as they had taken all the food to the hospital; they were swollen from starvation and too weak to move. Nothing could save them now.

Hunger and typhus were spreading in the ghetto. The notice: *Fleckfieber, Eintritt verboten,* was on almost every gate. The frontier between life and death was lost in the slow agony. On the streets, in the melting snow, people lay, some still begging for bread, others inert, like logs of wood, swollen and silent. Their eyes were hollow, their arms and legs bloated. Pus seeped from their infected sores. Though a spark of life still remained, the body was already decomposing. The corpses were covered with newspapers. Printed pages marked the gradations of death. The cemetery was overflowing. The Germans took over a nearby sports stadium as an additional burial ground. The number of dead rose to 300 per day. The Jewish cemetery grew, the Jewish ghetto shrank.

The streets were drowned in the mud of the melting snow. The courtyards were befouled with accumulated filth. Every few days the water supply grew worse. Diseases of various kinds, especially typhus, spread with the greatest rapidity; the hospitals filled up until there was no more room.

In the empty flat Hoppy and his sisters were dying. They looked more like skeletons dressed in rags than living children. Nothing could have saved them from death had they not managed one night to break out of their apathy and crawl towards the ghetto walls. In the darkness, they found a hole letting out the overflow from the sewers and with a supreme effort they pushed through to the Aryan side.

German patrols combed the district. But the children were indifferent to danger; death was for them a game, to be met face to face. They crawled to Kerceli Square and fell asleep amongst the market's stalls. They awoke to see an elderly woman leaning over them with a cup of hot coffee and a slice of bread in her hand. With great difficulty, they managed to swallow some of it. Later on that day, others took pity on them and offered food and money. In the evening the three children returned to the ghetto carrying a load of crusts.

Next day they went out again. They made the rounds of houses, begging. Sometimes they would get a piece of bread or a plate of hot soup, sometimes they were simply pushed out without a word. There were even occasions when they were chased away with shouts of "Get out of here, Yids!" They shrugged their shoulders and moved on, through the length and breadth of the town, learning their way around, hoping to get a better reception at the next house. Daily at the same time they would cross Marszalkowska Street where they would sit in some gateway and eat a part of the bread they had begged. Afterwards they would return to their 'work'.

Every day their fear lessened, and gradually they acquired the skills necessary to avoid danger. They became friendly with a group of Jewish children who also brought food to the ghetto. Some days when the going was dangerous for the three of them, they would cross the wall together and afterwards separate, and in the evening meet again beside the wall, where the elder sister would watch out for them.

One day, a German soldier, recognising Hoppy on Chlodna Street, hit him with the butt-end of his rifle. The boy fell unconscious, his face covered with blood. When he came to, he was in the ghetto. A Jewish *riksha* was taking him to hospital. Once his wound was dressed, he was escorted back home. There was no room in the wards.

Hoppy's sisters continued with their exits to the Aryan side. Once they entered the doorway of 16 Krucza Street in order to eat there the soup which a Polish woman gave them. Suddenly the concierge came out, an old woman of 60, stooping, grey-haired, a stick in her hand, and a bunch of keys hanging from her belt. She looked like a witch. The children took fright, abandoned their eating utensils along with the soup and started to run away.

"Don't be frightened, children! I won't harm you!" cried the old woman. The children came back and she said: "Take your soup and come to my house."

They entered her house, looking intently around the place. The walls were covered with spiders' webs, the floor was filthy black. Above could be seen an attic or gallery full of junk. In front, by a small window, stood a little table covered with a fairly clean cloth and on it stood a statue of the Blessed Virgin and a vase of artificial flowers. Below was a dirty couch, supported by some bricks, which a lodger had thrown out into the courtyard. On the couch, among the rags, romped some rabbits, which were looked after by the concierge's imbecile daughter.

The girls sat at the table, drank their soup, and after thanking the woman for her hospitality, went quickly on their way.

A few days later they were caught in a storm. They looked around anxiously for a place to shelter from the blinding rain. One of the girls suggested returning to the concierge on Krucza Street. The old woman ushered them in and since there was no let-up in the rain, they remained at her place until evening.

"Where do you live?" the concierge asked them.

"Far from here, at Pelcowizna," the girls answered, trembling.

"If that's the case, sleep here. Go up to the loft and stay there until morning." She let down a ladder, and the girls climbed up. Happy at finding a shelter, they gave the concierge some zlotys. The old woman checked the money with surprise and afterwards added, "If it pours with rain again, and you've nowhere to go, come to me."

And so they did. On the days they could not succeed in returning to the ghetto, they would go to Granny's in Krucza Street. Until one Wednesday, the 22nd July, 1942.

On that date the death sentence was passed on the ghetto. Posters announced that all 'unproductive' Jews were to be resettled in the East. The beggars were the first to go; then the refugees from small towns who occupied special centres. Then the children from institutions and orphanages. Many of the little smugglers, who were caught at the ghetto walls, went on those early transports. Thousands were driven daily to the *Umschlagplatz*, the 'place for the handing over of freight', and from there to Treblinka.

One of Hoppy's sisters, Basia, was on the Aryan side at the time. After a few days Hoppy, too, managed to escape from the ghetto. Every evening when the blockade was lifted he returned to the barbed wire on Zelazna Street, and surreptitiously threw some bread to his sisters who were still inside. Unable to leave the ghetto, they hid in cellars and attics. Finally, hungry and exhausted by constant hounding, they decided to give themselves up. Those who volunteered for the Umschlagplatz were given three loaves of bread and a ration of jam, and at first many people driven by hunger reported to the trains, unaware that it meant death.

In this way, Hoppy and his sister remained alone on the Aryan side. They wandered through the town and good people gave them food and money. Nights presented the greatest difficulty. They would spend their nights in destroyed buildings, attics, or amongst ruins. Every few days they would sleep in Krucza Street at Granny's. But none of these was safe for long—even the ruins could not be used too often—lest they should be seen and the police notified. Days passed. The damp cellars and cold attics brought on an attack of rheumatism and Hoppy began to limp.

Then, one day, the two children met another boy, whom they had known during their smuggling days in the ghetto.

This was the 13-year-old Conky. The weight of loneliness proved greater than their fear, and after some hesitation they approached him. They told each other about their experiences and about the death of their families. (Conky's parents and two brothers had died of hunger.) They decided to hunt together. Their first joint venture took them to the back door of the bar at Widok Street. The cook brought out some hot soup and the children went up to the attic at 7 Widok Street to eat and to continue their talk. But suddenly the sound of footsteps on the stairs shattered this moment of relative peace. One of the tenants, hearing some suspicious whispers, was coming up to investigate.

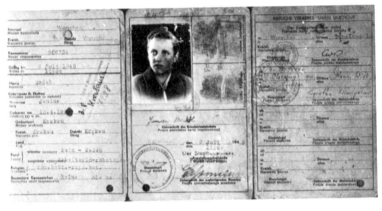

Jasia's false identity card

PROPERTY OF
BETH EL LIBRARY

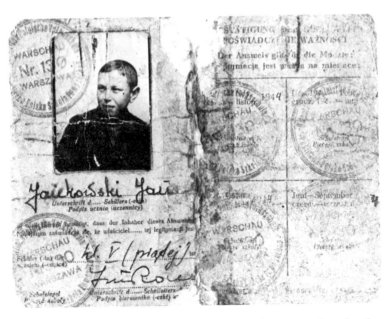

*School identity card supplied to one of the cigarette sellers by the
Jewish National Committee*

Mrs. Dargielowa of the R.G.O.   *"Grandma" Eva Broska*

Mrs. Lodzia provided a "den."

iv

At Mrs. Kalot's

"WHAT ARE YOU DOING HERE?" A frightened silence. Then the woman, who was watching them closely, understood.

"Come to my place, you can eat there at the table," she offered.

Conky got up from the floor and, unwillingly, the other two followed. The Polish woman lived in the attic. Slowly, full of fear and suspicion, the children entered the small, beautifully clean room. Ther were some flowering plants on the window sill; in the centre stood a table covered with a clean cloth. A picture of Christ hung on a wall with a small lamp burning before it. The woman poured coffee made from rye into mugs and cut some bread on a plate.

"You are little Jews, aren't you?"

The children, taken by surprise, shook their heads in denial.

"Don't be scared, I don't mean to harm you. I knew many Jews before the war, they were very decent people. They are probably dead now."

The children listened, unbelieving and still half-afraid, but gradually gaining confidence, as the woman made clear her own loneliness.

"I can see you are all right; if you have nowhere to sleep you can stay here."

The unexpected invitation filled them with joy. The woman heated some water—it had been so long since they had had a good wash with hot water. She made up a bed on the floor, far more comfortable than their last beds at home. Tired out after their wanderings, they fell into a deep sleep. Early next morning the woman woke them up. They found coffee with real sugar on the table and bread on a plate. They gobbled avidly.

"I could stay in to look after the house," offered Hoppy's sister, Basia, who was afraid of going out. The woman agreed. The two boys thanked her for her hospitality and gaily ran down stairs. The woman called after them: "Come back when it's dark, only take care no one sees you!"

In the entrance, they stopped to examine the list of tenants. Conky quickly ran his finger down the index.

"Here," he whispered. "Attic: Zofia Kalot, widow, employed in a German Mess." They looked at each other.

"Maybe she will betray us?" began Hoppy.

"Stupid, she could have already," said Conky decisively.

"But . . . ."

"What are you afraid of?" interrupted Conky. "You only die once!"

That evening, on her way home via Marszalkowska Street with a container full of soup, Mrs. Kalot noticed a little boy who sat begging under a wall not far from Wilcza Street.

"You must be hungry," she said.

The child did not answer, but raised his head fearfully. She had no doubt that he was Jewish.

"Come with me, I'll give you something warm to eat," she said, taking his hand.

He looked around, frightened, but went with her. When they arrived at her home, Basia was at the door and called out to the woman; the child turned white with fear and backed away, trying to escape.

"Don't be afraid," Basia told him.

The two boys arrived a few minutes later and pounced on the child. Conky grabbed his hands.

"Remember how we crossed the wall together . . . what's your name?"

"I am Bolus," said the child when his first fears abated.

"Leave him be, let him eat. Come to the table all of you," ordered Mrs. Kalot, ladling soup on their plates.

After dinner the children went to bed but could not sleep. They showered Bolus with questions, anxious for news from the ghetto.

"Is anyone from your family still there?" asked Conky.

"No—Mummy, Daddy and one sister died before the action, I stayed with my three elder sisters. When the action began we hid in the flat. We piled a table and all the chairs against the door so that they couldn't get in, but the police broke in and dragged all of us out to the courtyard. There were lots of people there. They all had some papers. We didn't have any so they pushed us into a crowd on the street. A Ukrainian fired with his rifle. We went through Zamenhoff Street. My sisters were trying to push me out, to make me run away, but I didn't want to. Near Kupiecka Street they pushed me out altogether and I hid around the corner. They all went on and I was left alone. I went to the hospital on Zelazna Street where my eldest sister was working and I sat two hours in a coal bin there. I saw the Ukrainians pulling people out of beds and killing them. There was blood everywhere. I couldn't stand it so I ran away. At the corner of Krochmalna Street I hid between some barrels. I don't know what happened then because I fell asleep. When I woke up next morning there was no one about, only lots of feathers and things. I didn't want to stay there, so I jumped through the barbed wire and ran. I wandered through the streets where kind people gave me food, and . . . here I am."

"But I want to be with my sisters, who went over the Bug," he added after a moment of thought. (The Jews 'resettled' from Warsaw were told that they were going to work in the East of Poland, beyond the River Bug.)

"You won't find them now; better stay with us," advised the children.

They talked late into the night, filling the little room with smothered whispers until finally sleep overcame them. In the morning they were awakened by Mrs. Kalot.

"I'm going to work now. I'll be back in the afternoon. You can stay here, only keep quiet—no one must hear you. If anyone knocks, don't answer." The children were about to reply, but she continued. "There's food on the table; if you want more, there's some bread in the cupboard."

"But we want to go back to the ghetto," said Basia.

"For the time being you'd better stay here. You'll go when things get better."

She left, padlocking the door from the outside. The children remained in their corner the whole day, talking in half-whispers. Every now and again Bolus would go to the window and survey the street, keeping carefully out of sight so that no one could watch him from the house opposite. Mrs. Kalot returned at 4 p.m., bringing a billy-can of soup.

Days passed. One day Mrs. Kalot took Basia with her to help carry the shopping. They went to the market, the young girl carrying the parcels. Suddenly, in the crowd, she saw a friend with whom she often used to go to the Aryan side from the ghetto. "Teresa!" she cried. With great difficulty they resisted the impulse to embrace. It was better not to attract attention.

Teresa was 14 years old. She was pale, with hollow eyes, and wore a man's jacket and a patched skirt. Her eyes surveyed the basket of food, somewhat suspiciously.

"What are you doing? I see you've got a den," she whispered, unable to tear her eyes from the basket of food. "Take me with you," she begged. Hoppy's sister looked at Mrs. Kalot who was approaching from one of the stalls as if to say: it all depends on her.

Mrs. Kalot looked suspiciously at the new girl, whose eyes were pleading.

"I'll help you, Madam, I'll do anything. I've got nowhere to sleep," she whispered, half-crying, before the Polish woman could say a word. For a moment the three stood silently.

"Take that parcel," said Mrs. Kalot finally. In a short while the three of them were back at Widok Street.

"Hey, where are you?" called Mrs. Kalot as she entered the seemingly empty room. The three boys peered from behind the wardrobe.

"What sort of a game do you think you're playing?" said Mrs. Kalot, somewhat angrily.

"None, Madam; we got scared when we heard a strange voice," explained Hoppy.

Teresa greeted the boys and told them how she had come upon the others.

"Perhaps tomorrow the ghetto will quieten down and you will be able to return home," Mrs. Kalot consoled them.

But days passed and the resettlement did not end. On the contrary, the action was becoming even more widespread. Mrs. Kalot brought sad news from the town. The children got fed up waiting for the action to end and began going out again. They went from house to house, begging for food, as Mrs. Kalot was too poor to feed them constantly. They left early in the morning, separately, so as not to arouse the suspicion of the janitor. If they met accidentally in town they never spoke but went on as if they did not know each other. Only occasionally did they dare to wink.

New Friends

ONE RAINY AUGUST day Conky was walking down Chmielna Street when he noticed a group of Jews marching, hunched in the downpour. Rain streamed down their torn overcoats. An armed German harried the last ranks, driving them on. "I wonder who they are," thought Conky, and decided to follow. They turned into the entrance of No. 67 and into the German wood store of Omnium. Several Poles, men and women, waited in the street outside; they had come to do business with the Jews. For the price of a few shillings or for food, unobtainable in the ghetto, the Poles bought clothes or any other articles that the Jewish workers might have managed to smuggle out. The bargaining was done in sign language, each gesture indicating an item of clothing or its value. The business concluded, the Jews threw the clothes into the street. Only occasionally did one of them manage to squeeze through a hole in the fence, or to bribe the sentry and approach the Poles personally.

At first Conky kept in the background, observing the scene. Then, sidling up to the fence, he looked inside. The vast square was filled with stacks of wood, planks and logs. Dozens of Jews ran to and fro, carrying planks to the railway trucks waiting on the siding. The German overseer cracked his whip, yelling, "Verfluchte Juden, schneller, los!"

42

That evening, Conky returned home and told the others about the Jewish workers. The following day everyone except Basia went along to Chmielna Street. The Polish pedlers were there again and as soon as one of the workers got out they pounced on him.

"What have you got? Show us! How much?"

The children tried to reach the Jew, to ask him about the ghetto, but the buyers wouldn't give way, busily haggling and inspecting the merchandise. Little Bolus tried to slip in between their legs with a polite 'Excuse me, please', but he stepped on someone's foot and immediately there was an indignant shout of "Where are you going to, blasted Jewboy?" followed by a kick. The boy returned in tears to the other children who were standing at the side.

For about an hour they continued to wander about the place. Suddenly, a young Jewish worker, not much older than the children themselves, noticed them in their torn rags of clothing and, realising that they were Jews, approached.

"What are you doing here, where are you from?"

"We've run away from the ghetto; they've taken everyone; we sleep at a Polish woman's house," said Teresa all in one breath.

"Come inside," the young man invited them. The children were afraid of the Germans but their new friend reassured them. They went in with him through a hole in the fence and were immediately surrounded by other workers, searching for familiar faces. Questions rained from all sides. Where were they from? How did they get out? Were they hungry? And the children in turn asked questions about the ghetto.

Suddenly there was a cry of "Zex!"—a sign of approaching danger. The workers ran in all directions, but the young man stopped a moment and pointed to a wood stack that had been thrown on the ground.

"Hide there! I'll be back!" He grabbed a couple of planks and carried them to the railway truck under the eyes of an approaching German. The children crouched together, trembling with fear.

"Don't worry, Bolus," Hoppy tried to reassure himself as well as others. "That 'bull' there will look after us." Bull seemed a fitting name for their new friend, who appeared strong and tough in comparison with themselves. The nickname was to stick for good.

When the Germans walked away, Bull returned with 150 zlotys collected from among the workers.

"Come tomorrow afternoon. When the Germans go away you'll get some soup," he whispered.

The children slipped out, happy that they had found some Jews and a new protector. In the evening they returned to Mrs. Kalot loaded with bread and potatoes and with some money still in their pockets. They told the woman about their meeting, about Bull and all that happened to them. Teresa took the money from her pocket and put it on the table. Suddenly there was a knock on the door. Silence. Mrs. Kalot, pretending there was no one in, did not move. The unknown visitor knocked once more and went away. This unexpected visit threw a slight chill on their happiness but the children still felt that it had been a good day.

The following morning they again left the house separately and met in front of the woodyard. At 12 o'clock, when the lunch bell rang and the Germans went to their canteen, the Jews queued with their lunch pails in front of the kitchen. Bull looked outside, saw the children and let them in. They were given food and afterwards the workers brought out their presents: there was a shirt, a jacket, a pullover and some bread. The children wandered around the yard until the Germans returned and then they had to run.

They came back to the woodyard every day, feeling that they had found elder brothers or parents. Bull became their chief protector, and the food, money, and oddments they received, they would bring to Mrs. Kalot.

Once a Polish policeman stopped Teresa and Hoppy as they were walking in Chmielna Street. Teresa succeeded in escaping from his clutches and running away, but her friend was seized by the collar and dragged towards the police station.

The boy burst into tears and begged to be let go, even kissing the policeman's hand; then turned to grappling with him and tried to break away, but without avail. His heart almost stopped in fear. Teresa ran as fast as she could to the Jewish workers and told them about the disaster. The workers could think of nothing, until one of them suddenly said: "Let's bribe Wolf; only he can save him."

Two Jews hurried to Wolf's office—he was a German officer. One of them ostentatiously placed a gold ring on his writing desk. Hearing what they wanted, at first he was adamant in his refusal to help. Meanwhile a small group of workers had gathered in front of the office. Another worker handed another valuable to the German. Wolf softened, put the objects that were on the table into his pocket, and went into the street accompanied by one of the workers. Teresa led them, a few steps ahead on the other pavement.

The policeman, who had hold of the shaking child's collar, had reached the crossing of Zelazna Street. Teresa hastened her steps until they overtook them. "What's the matter?" shouted the German. "He's a Jew," replied the policeman. "Good, come with me," said the German. He seized the boy's hand and began to lead him back. The boy could not understand the excitement, kept glancing sideways and trying to escape. Teresa and the Jewish worker, walking behind, made signs to him to calm him. Eventually they arrived back at the yard and the German let the boy go, threatening to kill him if he fell into his hands again.

At the beginning of September 1942 the Germans organised a general expulsion. Between Lubecki, Gesia, Zamenhof, Mila and Stawki streets, and Parisow Square, they made the famous 'boiler', a totally enclosed space in which every single street was shut off, and all the remaining Jews were brought together to report for 'selection'. Only those doing especially important work for the Germans, in the Gestapo, SS, the *Ostbahn,* and in the factories inside the ghetto were exempt from this rule; and even some of them were taken and sent to Treblinka. By the middle of September the main action in the ghetto was over. Only about 50,000 so-called 'productive' Jews remained. But even they were in danger, living from day to day.

Some days after the selection Teresa began to beg the Jewish workers to take her with them into the ghetto. She had to see if any of her family remained. They explained to her that it was impossible, that it was dangerous, that the guard at the gate checked everything. But the girl would not be prevented. The workers bought her equipment from the Poles and the whole group set out for the ghetto, with Teresa among them. By the guard post at the ghetto entrance hundreds of Jews were already waiting. They were only allowed to take soup and a loaf of bread into the ghetto, although sometimes permission was given to take in a few potatoes. Some policemen would not give permission for anything, and would spill the food on the ground as the Jews filed past. They were helped in this by Polish and Jewish policemen. In order to bring in more valuable goods such as butter, bacon, ham, etc., faster and more subtle methods were needed; but above all a little bit of luck was required, and more than anything else the Jews and the Poles were at one in believing in this luck.

From both sides the houses looked down with rows of dead eyes. An uncanny emptiness pervaded everything. The workers reached Gesia Street, where another sentry guarded the passage from the so-called 'wild' ghetto to the central one.

Teresa went to the house on Wolynska Street where she had lived before the action. The notice on the door said: "Workers of the Ursus factory". Teresa stood on the threshold. There were strangers inside.

"Who are you looking for?" asked someone.

"Mother and father. We used to live here." No one answered. Teresa understood and burst into tears. In the morning she joined the working party going to the Aryan side. At the gate they passed a guard post. One policeman touched her shoulder, ordered her to take off her shoes and looked inside them. With the whip which was in his hand he lifted up her dress.

"All in order, forward!" he growled.

The group of workers including Teresa passed in step through the streets of the town, with two German *Werkschutz* guards over them.

The Omnium group reached Chmielna Street, where the other children were already waiting by the entrance.

"Well? What happened? they asked. Teresa did not move.

"There is no one," she said slowly. "No use going back." Sorrowfully the children went back to town to look for 'work'.

Winter came and with it frost. The children, dressed and shod by the workers, did not feel the cold too badly. Mrs. Kalot installed a little iron stove, which grew red-hot on a few pieces of coal and spread pleasant warmth in the room for when they returned from the day's work. But warmer than the stove and the soup or coffee heated on it were the smile and kind words of the woman. Every day they told her in detail how they had spent their time and what had occurred in the woodyard. Bull, whom the children told about Mrs. Kalot, sent her gifts: an aluminium kettle, a frying pan, a set of tea-spoons, a rather nice china jug.

In the ghetto such objects were still rolling around among the rubbish in the flats and yards, and the Germans did not prevent them being taken out. Polish pedlars paid a few groszy for them, but Bull rushed to give what he could find as a present to the woman.

In the middle of January 1943 the Germans began surrounding individual houses and even whole streets on the Aryan side. They collected the inhabitants, packed them into covered lorries and drove them out into the unknown. Fear also gripped the Jews inside the ghetto.

"If they are catching Poles, we are sure to get it too," they said, awaiting a new disaster. They were not wrong. On the 18th January, 1943 the second 'resettlement action' began. There was a renewed hunt for those hiding in cellars and attics. Some of the Jewish workshops outside the ghetto were closed, among them Omnium, whose workers were sent to the Umschlagplatz. Again, thousands were driven to the trucks going to Treblinka. The first armed encounter between Jews and Germans took place on Mila Street. The action ended after four days. The children, unable to find their friends from Omnium, returned to their old profession.

Police! Open up!

THE CHILDREN TOOK TURNS to stay at home during the day so as to guard the flat. When Conky's turn came he took the opportunity to patch up his trousers. Suddenly there was a knock at the door. The boy sat still, not answering. After a moment someone began manipulating the lock and even before Conky had time to put on his trousers, the door opened, revealing a young man. Surprised to see the boy, the intruder at first hesitated, then changed his mind and stepped inside.

"Good morning. I've come to look over the flat. I hear it is to be let," he began nervously.

Conky, realising the man was a common thief, regained his composure. "Would you mind waiting a moment? I've got an awful tummy-ache. I'll have to go downstairs." But instead of going to the lavatory on the next floor he ran down to the caretaker. The latter immediately sent for the police and closed the gate. Meanwhile the unsuspecting thief collected all the more valuable objects from the flat, hid them under a washbasin on the staircase and confidently walked down to the entrance—only to be met by a policeman. A quick search and recovery of the stolen goods defeated all his attempts at explanation. Conky became the hero of all the curious tenants.

When Mrs. Kalot returned home and heard about this she brought out a hidden pot of jam and they celebrated his triumph. That evening they talked exclusively about the thief. Basia and Hoppy praised Conky's courage, his cleverness and coolness.

"Mrs. Kalot won't throw us out now: Conky showed her what we can do." But Teresa advanced some very unchildlike objections: the whole house had seen Conky, someone might give him away; and anyway why did they have to call the police?

The following day brought confirmation of her fears. A policeman called several times to question Conky, and left a summons when he found that the boy was out. Conky was the principal witness of the affair, but it was quite out of the question that he should show himself at the station. There was no solution except to leave. Despite her brother Hoppy's opposition, Basia left with Conky and went to stay with another Polish woman, Mrs. Urban at Grojecka Street, whom she already knew and where she was allowed to sleep for a small payment. The woman seemed kind at first and the girl told her the whole sad story.

Mrs. Urban raised chickens which she sold at the market. Her supplementary—or rather chief—income came from the rent paid by a young Jew, Mietek, from whom she extorted an ever-increasing ransom. Mrs Urban often said to the girl: "The Jews have money. You, I keep for half-price, so let him pay for you both."

Mietek, worked the whole day as a caretaker's helper in one of the houses at Jerozolimskie Avenue and got only his keep in return. He tried to explain that he had no more money, having sold all his possessions, but the landlady remained merciless.

"All Jews say they haven't got money, but if you look closely you always find some." And she once told the girl: "I'm risking my neck for that mangy Jew and he's trying to pull the wool over my eyes. If he doesn't pay I'll denounce him."

Warned by the girl, Mietek vanished. He hid in various attics but was discovered by Mrs. Urban and denounced to blackmailers, after which he vanished without trace. As for the girl, her comparative peace and security in the new lodgings did not last much longer. Mrs. Urban, suspecting that the girl had played some part in Mietek's disappearance, began threatening her too, so she had to go in her turn. Tired out after several days' wandering in town, and afraid of Mrs. Urban's vengeance, she decided to leave Warsaw and try to find work on a farm. She too vanished without trace.

Conky spent his first few nights in the attic. One night, when the bitter cold completely prevented him from sleeping, he wandered from place to place, but even in the lumber-covered corners of the attic he could not find protection from the wind. Suddenly an idea flashed through his mind. He began searching for all the doormats he could find and took them to an attic. In a corner he prepared a place for himself and immediately fell asleep.

He awoke in bright daylight. From the stairs came agitated female voices: "My doormat's gone?" "Mine too!" "Look what we've come to, they're stealing dirty doormats now!"

Conky waited until the voices had died down, then quickly ran down the stairs leaving the doormats in their right places. For the time being he continued to sleep in the ruins; but one day, hearing from the other children that the police had stopped calling, he decided to return to Mrs. Kalot. Life continued normally. Conky wandered the streets: Bolus begged from house to house. Teresa and Hoppy went every morning to the sentry post to wait for the Jewish work groups leaving the ghetto. The workers gave the children money and various smuggled items. Sometimes the children were stopped by schmalzers and had to save themselves by running away or paying up.

On Sunday morning, Conky and Bolus set out to town for their day's work. Teresa and Hoppy decided to stay in the flat. They were sitting at the table talking, when there was a sharp knock on the door. Silently, Mrs. Kalot pointed to the coal-hole. Two more knocks shook the door, followed by a kick.

51

"Open up! Police!" cried a man's voice. Mrs. Kalot opened the door. Three tough-looking civilians burst into the room. The so-called police turned out to be blackmailers. Mrs Kalot turned pale.

"You're hiding Yids!" thundered one of the visitors.

Mrs. Kalot tried to deny it, to convince them they were mistaken, but they would not listen.

"We know everything. People have seen them. Do you know Mrs. Urban who sells chickens?"

Would Hoppy's sister betray her own brother? wondered Mrs. Kalot—for it was clear that Mrs. Urban, before whom Basia had mentioned the Kalot home, had denounced them to the blackmailers.

"But gentlemen, what do you want from me?"

"What do we want? You know how to take 100,000 zlotys per head and you pretend you don't understand," replied one of the men.

"We also want to live," added the second.

"So you still don't know what we are after?" asked the fat, well-dressed leader. "Let's search the place!" he ordered.

They began inspecting the tiny flat. They looked in the wardrobe, under the bed, in the chest of drawers, passing by the coal-hole where the children crouched holding their breath. The slightest sound would have given them away. But the blackmailers did not open the coal-hole.

"The good Lord must have covered their eyes," said Mrs. Kalot later. The men, not finding anyone, left, promising to return.

But on their way from the house they ran into Conky, returning home.

"Here, boy." One of the men caught up with him. "We know you are Jewish. Don't be afraid, we don't mean any harm, but you've got to tell us where the rich Jews live."

"What Jews? I'm not a Jew," protested Conky. The blackmailers dragged him into the entrance hall and to confirm the truth pulled down his pants.

"You filthy Yid, want to lie to us, eh?"

They searched his pockets and took the money he had earned that day. Then they took off his jacket and pullover. Conky burst into tears.

"Tell us where the Jews are and you'll get everything back. And a pair of good boots. But if you don't we'll take you to the Gestapo and you'll get a bullet in the head."

Weeping, Conky begged them to let him go.

"Stop screaming, or you'll cop it," threatened the leader.

"Well, are you going to talk?" added the others.

Conky did not answer. The blackmailers began dragging him towards the police, threatening: "They'll get it out of you there." Conky, seeing that he was in serious trouble, made one last desperate effort.

"Listen," he stammered, "I'll find out today where there are Jews and tell you tomorrow."

The men, realising they would not get any more for the present, decided to let him go.

"If you don't come tomorrow, we'll deal with you next time," was their parting threat.

Conky walked away slowly, gradually increasing his pace, and remembering he must not look back. Once round the corner, however, he ran as fast as he could. In a roundabout way he returned to Widok Street and, seeing nobody suspicious, went back to Mrs. Kalot. Teresa and Hoppy sat at the table still frightened. A moment later Bolus appeared.

Panting, Conky began his story.

"We've had a scare too," interrupted Teresa.

"You must go away, children. They may come again," pleaded Mrs. Kalot nervously.

The children conferred in a corner. "We will go tomorrow morning," decided Teresa, the eldest. Only Bolus did not understand what had happened and refused to go; he looked pleadingly at Mrs. Kalot.

At dawn, the children got up from their bed and Teresa ran to the window.

"Time to go. It's late."

Mrs. Kalot went downstairs to check if the gate was open

and the road clear. The children thanked her warmly for the help and care she had given them and kissed her hands. Mrs. Kalot wept, then opened a trunk and took out the birth certificate of her dead daughter Sylvia.

"Take it, it may come in useful," she said to Teresa, who did so and hid it away.

And, as they were leaving, she followed them out, warning: "Be careful, look after yourself. Teresa, take care of Bolus!"

And she made the sign of the Cross over their heads.

The children went down slowly, so as not to arouse the neighbours' suspicion. They went without knowing where; four small figures creeping along in the shadow of the houses.

Children of the Streets

THE WHOLE OF THAT DAY the children wandered through the town. People passed them with indifference, sometimes throwing them a slice of bread. Darkness fell and they still had nowhere to go. The curfew approached as they searched desperately for some shelter for the night. They went along Jerozolimskie Avenue, passed the bridge and reached the Saska Kepa quarter. Here they stopped at a ruined house and crept quietly into the cellar, feeling in the dark for a place where they could sleep unnoticed. Eventually they lay on the floor, tired out after their long walk, and quickly fell asleep. Thus for a short while they forgot the terrible reality. In the morning they were again faced with the same question: what now?

"You must get out of Warsaw," Teresa advised Conky. "The shmalzers know you and you'll be in trouble if they see you again."

So Conky went to the market where peasants sold food brought in from the villages. He went from one to another asking, "Do you need a boy to look after your cows?"

After several hours he found a farmer from the Radzymin district who agreed to take him for his keep only. Conky haggled a bit, so as not to arouse suspicions.

"Give me a few zlotys, mister, and I'll come. I live with my uncle but we've had a row and I'm scared to go back."

55

But the farmer wouldn't agree and in the end Conky accepted his terms. He climbed into the cart and they moved on. At sunrise next morning, Conky took the cows to graze. Waving a stick, he sang all the Polish songs he knew, feeling safe and free. There were no Germans here, nor the blue uniforms of the Polish police. He need not pretend to anyone that his father had been sent out to do forced labour in Prussia and his mother was in hospital. He was alone with the cows, as they quietly chewed grass. In the evening he brought them back and returned to the farm house where a large dish of potatoes and a mug of skimmed milk waited on the table.

In the meantime, Teresa, Hoppy and Bolus wandered around Warsaw, separately so as not to attract attention. They met in the evening to look for a new shelter. It was dangerous to sleep too often in the same place. And so the days passed.

One evening they went out to the allotments at Grochow, a quarter in the eastern part of Warsaw, and hid behind a wood-stack. It looked like a good hide-out, but very soon the moon vanished behind leaden clouds, the wind rose and the rain came. The planks knocked against one another, waking the children from their sleep. Finally the heavens opened. The water washed the ground from under their feet and the planks began to slip. The children, wet to the skin and trembling with cold, cuddled together, their clothes clinging to their bodies.

Towards morning the rain stopped and again they found themselves on the street, wondering where to go, where to dry their clothes and find some warmth. People were turning round to look at them.

"Let's go to Krucza Street. I know a woman there, a care-taker—Granny—she's a good sort, she used to let Basia in," proposed Hoppy. The plan was approved and off they went. They opened the door quietly and peered inside. The old woman was sitting motionless beside the table, a tin mug with soup which she brought from the R.G.O. kitchen in her hand.

Hoppy made himself known to the old woman and she allowed the children to rest and dry their clothes. They told her that they lived far away, that they had bad parents who beat them and took all the money they earned begging. They stayed on till the evening.

"It's getting late; you won't be able to go home now," said the old woman. Teresa shuddered at the thought of returning to look for shelter in the ruins. "And perhaps . . .?" she stuttered, unable to finish the sentence. To their good fortune the old woman finished it herself. "You can stay here and sleep in the loft, only don't wee on the floor." She brought out a ladder and the children climbed up, to sleep among the lumber and the rags.

In the morning the old woman woke them up. "Well, it's already time to come down." Teresa thanked her and slipped three zlotys in her hand. Glancing with evident pleasure at the money, the old woman hid it in her clothes. "Dear children, may you earn well today." She blessed them as they left. "If it starts to rain, or if it gets late again, you can come back here!" And this became the new pattern of their lives.

During the warmer April nights, the children slept in ruins or in cellars. When the weather turned cold and rainy, they returned to Granny's on Krucza Street. Gradually they went back more and more often.

One morning they were awakened by sounds of shooting. There was fighting in the ghetto. The children could not hide their anxiety; their souls were still behind the ghetto walls. Against Hoppy's advice and earnest pleas, Teresa decided to go to the wall of the burning ghetto. She stood among a watching crowd but was unable to stay long. With tears in her eyes, she boarded a passing tram, where her red eyes attracted someone's attention. "Get out, you bloody Jew!" he shouted, pushing her off with all his force just as the tram started. She fell out, cutting her head. Blood poured over her face and she lost consciousness. The tram did not stop. Teresa awoke in a hospital bed, after an operation—for she had a fractured clavicle as well as her cut forehead. But the most important fact was that no one had recognised her, and in spite of the pain, she felt quite well. She slept in a real bed, was sheltered from the rain and was even well fed. "Let's hope I can stay here as long as possible," she thought.

Slowly her health improved and she had to leave. She was feeling quite well again; only a large scar over her left eye remained as a reminder of human cruelty.

Teresa found herself again on the street. In the evening she went back to Granny. Nearing the house she heard someone calling her name.

"Teresa! Teresa! You're alive!" Hoppy and Bolus hugged her delightedly and all three entered the caretaker's room.

A few days later they were on their way to the R.G.O. kitchen on Bracka Street when Hoppy tugged at Teresa's sleeve. "Look! See those two girls on the other side? They are 'ours'. I remember them from the ghetto. . . ."

Two sisters, aged fourteen and nine, stood under a wall, singing Polish songs. The elder, an Aryan type, collected money from passers-by. The younger, looking obviously Semitic, attracted listeners with her clear voice. Her large, dark eyes awoke sympathy and compassion. Noticing Hoppy and Teresa, she winked and stopped singing. She quickly turned a corner and disappeared with her sister into the entrance of a house. Teresa and Hoppy followed.

"What are you doing? How do you live?" Teresa questioned the two girls.

"As you see, we sing in the streets," answered Marysia, the elder. "And in restaurants too," added Stefcia. "And we earn quite a lot, but the nights are difficult."

For many months they had wandered round the streets earning their living by singing. Their nights were spent with different women they met by chance. Because of Stefcia's Jewish appearance they had to change their place of sleeping continuously and at times fate caused them to sleep in the ruins. After a short while they got to know a 12-year-old Polish girl who brought them to her grandmother's house, where they used to sleep on the floor. The singing made them a profit which they gave to their friends, the Polish girl and her grandmother, for safe keeping.

Once Stefcia fell ill with typhus and inflammation of the lungs. The fever consumed her alarmingly, but they were frightened to call a doctor. The landlady was afraid the girl would die, and that it would be discovered that she had been hiding Jews. She requested firmly that the sick girl be taken outside, and Marysia's entreaties were of no avail. In this hopeless situation Marysia decided to take Stefcia in a cart to the children's hospital in Kopernik Street. There she dumped the child in front of the waiting room and ran off. When they found Stefcia and realised what was the matter with her they sent her to the hospital for infectious diseases in Wola. Three months passed before Stefcia returned cured to her sister, and they recommenced singing in the streets. They were so good that they received offers to appear in various taverns, one of which was the restaurant in Three Crosses Square—a very busy place, with underworld characters among its customers, and at times German soldiers.

"We too find the nights difficult," confided Hoppy. "Sometimes we've nothing to eat."

Teresa told the story of her encounter with the shmalzers and of her own accident, showing them her scar.

"You'll get caught if you go on like that," warned Stefcia. "There'll always be some louse ready to shop you. You know sometimes we sing at the Three Crosses Square? Some Polish boys there sell cigarettes to Germans and they seem to be doing quite well. Perhaps you could try it. You'd be quite safe there and it would be a good cover."

Hoppy hesitated; he was afraid of change. But Teresa caught on immediately.

"A wonderful idea," she decided.

A New Profession

IN THE AFTERNOON Teresa, Hoppy and little Bolus went to the
Three Crosses Square. On the way they bought a packet of
Swojak (home-made) cigarettes.

How to begin? Teresa looked around carefully. A few
Polish boys strolled in front of the *Soldatenheim* (Soldier's
Home) selling cigarettes.

"Wait here, I'll try over there," she said, indicating the
former Queen Jadwiga High School.

"Hey, what do you want here? Aren't the streets enough for
you? Get out, you and your rubbish!" yelled one of the Poles.

She returned to the two boys. "They won't let me stay there.
I'll try the railings of the Institute." Leaning back against the
iron rails she took out her cigarettes and waited for a client.
Hoppy hovered nearby, watching out for police and gendarmes.
Two drunken German soldiers came out of the Soldatenheim
and approached the photographer.

"*Du, mach eine Aufnahme!*" shouted one of them. Teresa
ran over with her packet.

"Zigaretten?"

The soldier pulled out a banknote, gave it to her and took
the cigarettes.

Teresa ran happily to the two boys. "I've sold them all!"

60

"You're joking," said Hoppy, astonished.

Teresa showed him the money. They hurried to Hoza Street to buy another packet. When evening came they were in possession of a tidy little sum. They bought a loaf of bread and went to spend the night at Granny's.

The next morning they returned to the Square. Now Hoppy too decided to go into business. Having found a few small planks in a rubbish heap, he cleaned them with a piece of glass and, using a brick for a hammer, joined them together. In a few minutes he had a tray which he showed to his companions:

"Look, I've made it myself!"

"Fix a bit of string to it so you can hang it on your neck," advised Teresa.

"Where can I get string?"

"Pull it out of your pants."

"But I'll lose them . . ."

"Well, you'll have to manage it somehow!"

Hoppy strolled round the square, finally stopping in front of the milliners. At the side of the shop window hung a long rope attached to the awning.

Just the thing, thought the boy. He wandered past the shop, and, when no one was watching, cut the rope with a piece of glass and ran back to Teresa.

"Look, I've got it!" He showed her his acquisition, then piling the cigarettes in his new tray, took his place beside her. Little Bolus, feeling slighted because he was not given any cigarettes, wandered off back to town. He stared at the well-stocked fruit shops and swallowed hungrily, drawing his fingers across the window-panes.

"Go on, scram!" the shop-owners chased him away. With a silent stare the child went on. He loitered aimlessly till he reached Solec Street under Poniatowski bridge, where a small crowd waited at the tram stop. Bolus looked around then leant against the Stop sign and began singing the only two songs he knew, *Jasiu krowki gnal* and *Chlopek Roztropek*. Starting softly, he soon gained confidence and went on, alternating the two simple children's songs over and over again. He was rewarded with small coins. In the afternoon he returned to the Three Crosses Square and proudly showed his earnings.

"Look how much I've got!"

The following day again he went under the bridge. This time he found a five-year-old Polish girl begging at the tram stop.

"Come with me, let's both sing together," he proposed. And added after a moment of thought: "If anyone asks, you are my sister."

Holding hands, the two children stood together at the tram stop and sang, with the result that they attracted a good deal of interest. But it did not last long: Bolus soon realised that quite a few people were looking at him too closely. So he persuaded his small partner to leave the stop and sing with him actually in the trams instead. From then on, they patronised the 'P' line and the passengers, taking pity, offered them money—except when the ticket-collector chased them off, as occasionally happened. At noon, Bolus and the girl jumped out of the tram on the corner of Ksiazeca and Czerniakowska Streets. Here, standing a little back from the street, was the Social Security Building. Wide concrete steps led to the main entrance, where the waiting-room was clearly visible through a glass door. The children sheltered there from the cold wind, while they waited for the next tram. The little girl looked rather boldly inside the waiting-room. A stream of warm air blew in her face. She motioned to Bolus and in a moment the two of them were sitting on the floor, next to the warm radiator.

Bolus emptied his pockets into his beret which he placed on his knees. The girl too emptied her pockets. They began to count.

"We've made 30 zlotys," said Bolus. "Here's your share." And he gave her half of the money, which she put in her pocket. Then, leaning against the radiator, they both fell asleep.

The passers-by pointed the abandoned pair out to one another. At length, the sound of the gasworks hooter announcing the end of the day's work woke them up.

"Come to the gasworks—you'll get some soup. I always get some there," proposed the girl. They crossed a courtyard and the girl opened the door and peeped into the kitchen.

"Come inside," called the cook. Bolus remained behind the half-opened door.

"Who's that?" the cook asked.

"He's with me," explained the girl.

One of the employees opened the door wide, letting Bolus in. He took off his beret. The cook filled two plates with soup and added a slice of bread to each. The children ate their meal, thanked the cook and went out. A sharp wind was blowing but they did not feel cold. Having arranged to meet the following day Bolus ran to the Square.

"Why are you so late? Where have you been the whole day? We thought something had happened to you!" scolded Teresa.

"I was sitting near a radiator in the Social Security."

"He's telling tall tales again," said Teresa to Hoppy, who came along at that moment.

Teresa and Hoppy felt completely at home at the Square. Business was going quite well and they earned several zlotys a day. Their chief worry now was Bolus, who disappeared for half a day at a time.

They took their dinners at the R.G.O. kitchen in Zorawia Street. They entered by the backdoor and the cook filled their billycans with soup. Afterwards they hid the dishes in the nearby bushes and returned to the Square. During that time another boy joined them—17-year-old Mosze, later called Stasiek, whom Hoppy knew from his smuggling days in the ghetto. He did not look very Aryan, but he was cheeky enough to confuse any shmalzer. His was an unusual story.

Some months before, he had escaped from the ghetto and began wandering the streets, unable to find shelter. One day, he was stopped by two rather well-dressed men. One of them introduced himself as Mundek, an agent of Kripo (the German Criminal Police), and demanded a large sum of money for not denouncing the boy to the Gestapo. Stasiek swore he had none.

"All right, you can make yourself useful then. You can point out rich Jews to us. We'll find you a place to sleep, we'll feed you and you'll want for nothing, as long as you work for us." So they threatened and tempted him at the same time.

The boy agreed, seeing no other way. They took him to Mundek's flat at 95 Marszalkowska Street and invited him to a table set with vodka and food.

"Give him a decent pair of trousers, let the Jew know he's got a good master!" Mundek yelled to his mistress. While Stasiek was changing his clothes, two Polish policemen entered the flat and the boy turned white with fear.

"Don't worry, they're with us," Mundek assured him, going into a huddle with the two men. After a short meal they all left the table.

"Now you've eaten, come on, let's see you work for those trousers," said Mundek, pulling him up by the shoulder. They went to the station of the suburban railway on Nowogrodzka Street and the hunt began. Mundek scrutinised the passengers boarding the trains.

"See that platinum blonde? I think she's a cat.* Go up to her and say a few words in Yiddish—and look her straight in the eyes," he ordered.

Stasiek did as he was told. The woman paled, her nervousness betraying an inner fear. This was enough for Mundek. He followed her into the train, took the adjoining seat and fixed her with a severe stare. The woman realised that she was being watched and left the train at the next station. Mundek jumped out through another door. She hastened her pace, then broke into a run. Mundek caught up with her in a few strides.

"Excuse me," he began politely, "would you mind stepping this way?"

"But why, what for?" she asked nervously.

"If you'd just step through this gate, I'll explain . . ."

"But what do you want? Please, tell me . . ."

"If you don't go in, you'll be sorry," he said, raising his voice and taking a few steps towards a nearby gendarme.

* Jews in hiding who pretended to be Aryans were called 'cats' by shmalzers.

"Please, sir," cried the woman, frightened. The blackmailer turned back and they entered a doorway.

"I think you know what this is about . . ."

"I am alone and I've no money. Have pity!"

"Too bad! In that case we'll have to take you to the Gestapo, and you know what will happen there . . ."

The woman trembled with fear. "I've got only 3,000 zlotys. It's all I have." She took the money from her handbag.

Mundek pocketed the bundle. "Not enough."

"But really, I've got nothing more; please, let me go," she begged.

"We'll see about that."

The blackmailer began to search her. He took a fountain pen and a pair of old-fashioned earrings from her handbag and demanded her gold wristwatch. He inspected her shoes, hoping to find something. Disappointed, he ordered her to take off her wedding ring.

"Now you can go."

The weeping woman dried her eyes and went on looking fearfully right and left.

She was not the only victim that day, and in the evening there was a party with plenty of drink at Mundek's flat. The blackmailers had obtained several thousand zlotys and many valuable objects, which Mundek showed his friends.

"My Jewish 'heritage'," he laughed. Then: "We've got to buy him some good boots," he told his mistress, pointing to Stasiek. "He's earned them."

After a time, when Mundek had earned a large fortune, Stasiek's help became no longer necessary. Now they were known, the victims ensured his monthly income. So Mundek decided to get rid of the boy and first of all took back his suit and boots. Stasiek, realising he was in danger, ran away from his 'protector'. He was still wandering the streets when he met Hoppy.

"Don't call me Mosze, my name is Stasiek," he warned, before even greeting the boy.

Hoppy took him to the Three Crosses Square and introduced

him to Teresa. After a few moments Bolus appeared and stared at the newcomer, hoping it was someone he knew.

"What are you staring at?" demanded Stasiek sharply and Bolus, hurt, stepped aside. Teresa laughed.

"Go to Hoza Street and buy 200 cigarettes so you'll have something to sell. Bolus, you take him there," she ordered.

A few hours later she went up to Stasiek, who was wandering round the Square, a packet of cigarettes in his hand.

"Well, how's it going?" she asked.

"Like blood from a stone," answered the boy, sulking, obviously not very happy in his new profession.

Teresa learned from one of the Polish boys that substitute cigarettes could be bought more cheaply at the Rozycki market in Praga, and they decided to investigate this new source of supply. The following morning they set out for the market. There they strolled amid the countless stalls, which sold everything: clothes, toys, footwear, gramophones, food, even German uniforms and guns. These last items were of course unofficial, available only to trusted customers. The children bought several hundred different cigarettes, all of them adulterated, and a few packets of real ones for special customers. Before leaving the market they stopped in front of a stall with a sign: 'Breakfasts, Lunches, Dinners'. A piece of paper in the window announced: 'Hot sausages', 'Hot tea'. Smoke billowed from the stove-pipe in the roof.

"Let's go in and eat something," proposed Hoppy.

There were two half-drunk cart drivers inside sitting at a small table with an overturned vodka bottle on it. The fat stall-owner stood behind her dirty, peeling counter.

"What will you have? Hot sausage? Tea?"

"Let's have both. Three portions," ordered Stasiek, like an old hand. "And don't forget the mustard!"

"Hey kids, how about a little glass? Come on, don't be shy," invited one of the drunks. Stasiek downed his in one gulp. His head spun. They ate quickly, paid and were walking out when Hoppy felt someone touch him lightly. He stopped and looked cautiously back. Behind him stood Bull from Omnium.

Bull—Leader of the Gang

THE EARLY CHILDHOOD of Ignacy—Bull's real name—was a happy one. Loving parents and a fairly high standard of living allowed him, even in the ghetto, to lead a relatively normal life. He played in the courtyard, attended lessons and never worried about his next meal. His father, an energetic man, had appraised the situation correctly early on and was among the first of the 'outside' workers. In this way, the family never lacked food.

The great action of July 1942 shattered this peaceful life. In the first days of the upheaval Bull's father was killed by a German gendarme who found a packet of saccharine on him during the search at the sentry post. Bull suddenly found himself the only man in the family. At this tragic moment, although only 15 years old, Bull showed a surprising energy and ability to cope. He established contact with other outside workers and through them exchanged clothes and other articles for food. He assumed the responsibility of providing for the family, bringing in their daily bread and potatoes and sometimes even sugar and fat. But one day he was seized in the street by a gendarme and taken to the Umschlagplatz.

There, Bull found himself among a dense crowd. The weeping of women and children drowned the voices of those calling for their families. Some tried to find temporary shelter in the only building there, but the slowly revolving door hampered their movements and the Jewish militiamen eagerly sought to maintain order. The gendarmes and Gestapo men drove them on to the trains with the aid of rifle butts and whips, and with bullets for those who fell behind. No one paid attention to the abandoned dead, or to the cries of the beaten mingling with the moans of the wounded. Everyone thought only of himself and of how to escape from the inferno.

The situation seemed hopeless, but Bull did not give up hope. The thought of his family would not leave him. In the initial confusion he managed somehow to avoid the clutches of the Germans. The first transport left and those who remained on the square had to wait till next morning for the arrival of new trucks. This was the time to act. Under cover of darkness, unnoticed by the watching SS men and Ukrainians, Bull scaled the high wall, returned to the ghetto and ran home as fast as he could.

He was met by wide open doors—a bad sign—but inside everything was in its place, dishes, furniture, even the china ornaments on the shelves.

"Mother!"

Dead silence answered his cry. For a moment he still hoped that she had gone out, looking for him perhaps, and that she would return. . . . Soon, however, he understood what had happened. His mother and three sisters had been taken to Treblinka. He was alone. What could he do now? Return to the Umschlagplatz? Would he find them there? And anyway, what happened to all would happen to him—perhaps.

A thousand thoughts whirled in his head, each darker than the last. However, he managed to overcome his misery and did not give in to despair. He decided to fight for his life, so as to be able to tell the world of the crime that was being perpetrated here. The only way to survive was to escape from the ghetto. But where . . .? It was a difficult decision. He was helped by a lucky break. A group of Omnium workers was waiting to be searched by the sentry. Without hesitation Bull joined the group and went out with them to the Aryan side. Once out he walked aimlessly around the town. Sometimes he was given suspicious looks, but he paid no attention. Everything here seemed different, strange; the people, the houses, even the trees. He looked around with indifference. The laughter of children irritated him, and would not let him in peace. He envied them. There—a sea of blood and tears; here—life, relatively normal. The wall divided two worlds.

Night was coming and Bull was faced with the problem of finding a shelter in a completely strange town. But where? To whom should he go?

His first plan took him to the house he lived in before the war. There he was welcomed with friendship and pity, fed, plied with advice and promises of help . . . perhaps tomorrow or next week. But no one offered a bed for tonight. That was dangerous. Death was the penalty for harbouring Jews. Bull decided to seek help from strangers and knocked at the door of a small house near a railway station.

"I've missed the train to Cracow. Could you put me up for the night?"

"It's probably a Jew," he heard in reply. It sounded like a curse, it hurt, reminding him that he had no right to live. What now? Should he return to the ghetto and try his luck again in a few days' time? He fought with this thought. Once defeated, he might not find the courage to fight again. He hid in the cellar of a strange house, only to be chased out by the caretaker. He tried to sleep among the market stalls, but was discovered by a German patrol who opened fire. It was only by a miracle that he escaped alive. Finally, exhausted and broken in spirit, he decided to return to the ghetto with the other workers. But the Omnium workshop was empty. Everyone had gone. The road back was closed too.

Bull felt helpless but did not cry. The approaching curfew left him little time to think. Finally he climbed over the fence and spent the night among woodstacks. Next day he rejoined the Omnium workers and gradually became one of them, returning to the ghetto by night; but his peace was shortlived.

Only a few days later all the Omnium workers were surrounded by Ukrainians and taken to the Umschlagplatz. Although they were eventually released, thanks to the intervention of the woodyard director, Bull remained, as he had no work permit. Thus, at length, he found himself on the train. The truck was jammed with over a hundred men, women and children. Some wept, others prayed, seeking Divine salvation or consolation, and yet others stood quietly, completely resigned and indifferent to their surroundings. The heat and stench were unbearable. The sun peeping through the little barred window seemed to mock them.

Bull decided once more to fight for his life. He broke the bars of the window with a plank. When the train slowed down at the curve near Zielonka he jumped out and rolled into a ditch. The Germans fired at him from the roofs and from inside the trucks but he escaped unhurt.

He hid in the forest and after many adventures got back to Warsaw. He returned to Omnium where the workers welcomed him with open arms. All of them liked him and his escape from the train added to the respect with which he was now treated. They managed to obtain a work permit and Bull became a regular labourer. He helped in the woodyard and bought food which was taken back to the ghetto. Bull knew how to bargain and had no difficulty in establishing contact with Poles who came to the fence. He was smart, courageous and honest and quickly gained the confidence of the workers, becoming the middle-man in their bargaining with Poles. He became particularly friendly with old Mrs. Janina Jakubisiak of 92 Chmielna Street and with a teacher from Grochow, Tadeusz Idzikowski, who lived in Stanislaw-August Street. They were among his regulars, exchanging 'merchandise' from the ghetto for food for the workers. Towards the end of August 1942, during one of his transactions, Bull noticed some children wandering about the street. Their appearance betrayed their origins. Bull left his business and approached the children. The Poles protested, wanting to conclude their haggling, but Bull replied, "I've no time today."

From that day on, the children—known to us already as Bolus, Teresa, Hoppy and Conky—found themselves under the care of the workers. They became extremely attached to Bull, little Bolus especially so. When, in January 1943, the Germans closed the workshop, Bull was no longer among the workers. He had escaped in time, feeling that one did not jump out of a train once only to find oneself in it again. The very same day he met some workers of the Ostbahn who were still useful to the Germans for unloading coal from trucks and repairing elevations. They welcomed Bull, who made himself helpful by cleaning their tools and bringing cigarettes and drinks. When one of the workers died, Bull was given his work permit. He began smuggling food to the ghetto. In principle, the workers were allowed to bring in only a loaf of bread or some potatoes. But some gendarmes threw out even that permission, and beat the men with rifle butts. One had to be very smart indeed to smuggle in butter, pork fat or sugar. Bull was fortunate, and not only in this respect.

By chance, in the ghetto he met an uncle, the only remaining member of his family, who put Bull in touch with the Resistance. At that time the Resistance were seeking to enlarge their arms market, and outside workers constituted one of the channels for this purpose. Among the Poles doing this business with the workers of Ostbahn was a Mr. Wroblewski, a tram-conductor from Chmielna Street and an acquaintance of Mrs. Jakubisiak's. Bull established contact with this man. At first, he bought only bread, but later on guns were smuggled in, in hollowed loaves. These arms were collected in the ghetto by the brothers Jasinski, and they passed them on to the Resistance. Bull was deeply impressed by his new role and took to it with enthusiasm in spite of the constant danger.

Every now and again Bull would stay for the night at Mrs. Jakubisiak's where he used to conclude his more serious transactions. It is difficult to say how far his activities would have developed had not the workers of Ostbahn been moved in March 1943 to barracks on the Aryan side from which they could no longer return to the ghetto. Their new home was a camp in Armatnia Street in the Wola quarter, where they were lodged in huts and surrounded by barbed wire. They were guarded by Ukrainians.

Bull, however, taking advantage of the initial confusion of this move, hid at Mrs. Jakubisiak's. But he could not remain there for any length of time. Too many people knew that he was a Jew. Mrs. Jakubisiak took him to a friend of hers, Mr. Wisniewski, a cobbler who lived also in Grochow at 31 Miszewska Street. After a great deal of persuasion, the cobbler agreed to take Bull on as his apprentice.

He began his new career by sweeping the floor and tearing soles off old shoes. It was a long time before he really began to learn the trade, but he was not worried. A roof over his head and a hot meal satisfied his ambitions as a cobbler's apprentice.

Passover was approaching and Bull decided to spend it with his uncle. On April 17th, 1943, he returned to the ghetto with a group of workers. The threat of final annihilation hung heavy over the remaining Jews. They were preparing to fight. Bull helped his uncle to construct a bunker and to dig a tunnel linking it with the neighbouring house. Two days later, on the night of the Passover *Seder,* the third action began and the ghetto rose to fight. Bull found himself among the fighters. When their ammunition was exhausted, the whole group took refuge in a bunker, but had to leave the following day when the Germans set their house on fire. They were rounded up, taken to the Umschlagplatz and herded into trucks which started rolling towards Poniatow.

There was another boy in Bull's truck, a 13-year-old Parisian named Kazik, and the two of them decided to escape together. Their moment came during a transfer to narrow-gauge track, but unfortunately Kazik was caught and taken back to the train. Bull alone managed to escape and, through little-used country lanes, to reach Pulawy. There he boarded a train for Warsaw and returned to Mr. Wisniewski.

And so he was once again pounding nails into old boots. In the middle of May he was accosted in a tram in Washington Avenue by a man standing next to him. Momentarily, his legs turned to jelly, but his fear vanished when he recognised Mr. Idzikowski, with whom he had 'worked' at Chmielna Street. They left the tram together. Mr. Idzikowski promised to help. And indeed, a week later, Bull received a school identity card.

At the beginning of June rumours of an impending blockade of Warsaw and search for hidden Jews spread through the town. In the ensuing panic, Mr. Wisniewski decided that Bull had to go.

"They'll kill us because of him," his wife lamented. Bull had to look for another shelter and again he turned for help to Mr. Idzikowski. After some thought and despite the danger, he agreed to employ Bull in the little shop he had opened in Michalin on the outskirts of Warsaw during the summer.

"Only remember, in case of trouble you'll say you came in answer to my ad." One more little lie in the sea of other lies, indispensable to the saving of one's life; it did not matter.

Bull spent his days running errands, sweeping the floor and making ice-cream. At night he guarded the shop, sleeping comfortably on a camp bed. Then one day Mr. Idzikowski sent the boy to Warsaw to do some shopping. Walking across Szembek Square Bull heard suddenly: "Hey, Jew-boy, let's have the cash!" Looking back, he saw two shmalzers.

"Well, how about it? Look, there are gendarmes coming . . . One more minute and we'll hand you over to them."

Bull looked round and saw that there was indeed a gendarme nearby. He began to run. The shmalzers followed. "Catch the Jew!" they cried. A crowd gathered, watching. Bull ran with all his strength. The suburban train for Karczew was passing and Bull jumped in. He struck the edge of a step and fell inside, his leg bleeding and hurting excruciatingly. Afraid of being followed, Bull left the train at the next stop, with the help of some passengers who did not realise what was happening. Leaning on a stick he managed to drag himself to the railway station at Wawer. There, no longer able to stand up, he stopped a passing cart which took him to Mr. Wisniewski in Grochow.

73

The cobbler seemed quite willing to keep the boy, but his wife, terrified, would not hear of it. Lying exhausted on the floor, Bull begged for help and pity. He realised fully that if they refused, he was lost. In the end, the cobbler prevailed over his wife. They hid Bull in the attic, where he spent two days in terrible pain. He asked to see a doctor, but Mr. Wisniewski was afraid to show him to anyone. Finally, when the pain became unbearable, Bull persuaded Mr. Wisniewski to take him to a woman doctor whom he had known in the past; it was his last chance.

They went to Sosnowa Street, where she lived, in a *drozki*. Mr. Wisniewski carried the boy to the door, rang the bell and hurried away. The doctor came out, but when she saw the boy and recognised him she immediately slammed the door shut again. Bull looked towards the entrance, but Mr. Wisniewski had vanished. This is the end, he thought, near tears. But he refused to give in. With his remaining strength he knocked again and after a few minutes the doctor opened the door. She was pale with fright. She explained that she could not possibly take him in, in case someone saw her and denounced her. The boy told her of his predicament and begged for help. Finally she relented and pulled him inside. She gave him an injection, dressed his leg and immobilised it in a temporary splint.

Bull had a cracked left shin and a deep wound in the ankle. On the following morning his leg was put in plaster. The wound was infected and the doctor changed his dressing daily, and also fed and looked after him. No one except her knew of his existence in the house.

A week later they were visited by the commandant of O.P.L. (Civil Anti-Aircraft Defence), who accused the doctor of hiding Jews. When she denied it he wanted to search the flat, but she managed to stop him. He left, promising to return with the police. Panic decended on the house. Strange people ran from room to room and it transpired that the doctor was in fact hiding several Jews. That morning they all ran away.

Bull thanked the doctor for her help and, staggering on his feet, left the house. He returned to Mr. Wisniewski, where he spent three days in bed and then decided to go back to his job in Michalin.

The Idzikowskis were as astonished to see him as if he had returned from the dead.

"What on earth happened to you? We thought you'd been caught."

Bull dismissed their questions with a gesture. Something else was on his mind. There was a strange boy in the shop. Bull understood. The camp bed was occupied—Mr. Idzikowski had taken on another helper. Bull had lost his shelter. He returned to Warsaw and wandered around not knowing what to do. He looked in at Rozycki's bazaar on Praga. That was when he met Teresa and Hoppy. The girl dropped her cigarettes in surprise and Hoppy was nearly in tears. They embraced. The children remembered well how he helped them on Chmielna Street. Now they could repay his kindness. They introduced Bull to Stasiek, who was with them, and the four of them hurried into the doorway of one of the houses.

"How are you? How are you earning your living?" asked Bull.

"We deal in cigarettes in the Three Crosses Square. Bolus is there too."

"Bolus too?" remarked Bull in an unusually tender voice.

"Come to the Square and see with your own eyes," invited Hoppy, and off they went.

The 'P' tramway was passing the Three Crosses Square and Teresa pulled Bull by the arm. They jumped on. Bolus and his little girl friend stood between the seats. He wore a torn fur coat tied with a piece of string. The girl looked a little tidier. They were singing. Bull observed Bolus and his eyes shone with pleasure. He wanted to approach but Teresa restrained him.

"Jump off and wait for us. I'll call him."

Approaching Bolus she nudged him gently. "Bull is here. The one from Chmielna Street."

Bolus left his friend and jumped off. In a minute they were embracing.

"Where were you all this time?" asked Bolus, near tears. "You'll stay with us at the Square?" he added, not waiting for an answer.

"Yes, yes, I'll stay, I'll work with you," promised Bull. His arrival at the Three Crosses Square was the start of a new life for the children. Bull had authority. In their eyes he was grown-up and experienced, and he became their leader.

Jurek (center) selling at Warsaw's Eastern Station, 1944

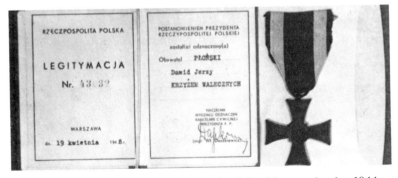

The Polish Military Cross Jurek received for his part in the 1944 Ghetto Uprising

Whitey (right) and other sellers (unknown) in front of a German restaurant, 1944.

Pawel (left) and Zenek, 1943.

In Granny's Loft

AT MIDDAY they all went to the kitchen at Zurawia Street, and in the evening they went to Krucza Street.

"Give us a zloty for medicine," Granny's backward daughter greeted them. The formalities over, they went up to the loft, lay down in the rags, among fleas and bed-bugs which would not let them rest. Yet all the same, it was a good den. They were warm and had little fear of being discovered.

The following morning the district policeman came to visit Granny and look at the lodgers' book. He inspected the place carefully.

"Whose children are those, up there?"

"My grandchildren, sir,"

The policeman checked the register, made some notes and left.

"And mind you keep the street clean or I'll fine you," he called.

The children, frightened by the unexpected visit, quickly left their lair. Half an hour later the whole group had gathered at Rozycki's bazaar. They bought cigarettes, ate their breakfast and went to the Three Crosses Square to work.

One evening, a few days later, they met another Jewish boy. This one looked typically Aryan, his fair hair falling over his

77

eyes resembling more an urchin from the banks of the Vistula than a past inhabitant of the ghetto. On that very day the boy had lost his den and was wandering the streets looking for shelter. When Bull saw him he asked hesitatingly, "Ours?"

"Yes, I know him," answered one of the boys shortly and with assurance. The cigarette sellers standing round about at first refused to believe it.

An hour later Jurek (as the new boy nicknamed himself) walked with the others to Krucza Street, to Granny's. Following the habitual 'procession' the children went up into the loft.

"When did you escape from the garden?" Hoppy asked Jurek, using the slang name for the ghetto.

Before the boy could reply, Bolus stopped him with a sudden question:

"Are you by any chance from Nowolipie?"

"He's starting with his Nowolipie again! Sit down and listen to how grown-ups discuss things," Bull rebuked him. Bolus shrank into a corner, insulted, and covered himself with his little fur coat.

"At the beginning of the war," Jurek began, "our family went to Otwock to the local ghetto. I used to smuggle food into Warsaw. I also took letters from Otwock to Warsaw and back. It went well enough. I earned a livelihood for the whole family."

"Huh, that's unusual!" sneered one of them.

"All of us were forced into the same position," added another. "Tell us what happened after."

The boy told his story and the cigarette sellers listened with interest. At the time of the action in the Otwock ghetto (in August 1942) his parents ordered him to escape. "You must save your life in order to preserve the family name," his father would say to him. Jurek saved himself at the right moment and fled to Warsaw to Polish friends.

One day he learned that there were Jews from the ghetto working in Narbutt Street. He began to take food there for the workers, and every few days he would go with them to the ghetto. There he met an acquaintance from Otwock, a Dr.

Levy, who was working in a resistance group. Jurek, who was denning on the Aryan side, became his messenger. Furthermore, he had in his hands large sums of money for buying arms. In the mornings Jurek, together with the Jewish workers, would cross over to the Aryan side and would receive arms in places that Dr. Levy indicated to him. He would take two or three revolvers, inside a knapsack, to 6 Muranowska Street, and hand them over to the caretaker; from there another messenger would take them to the ghetto through a tunnel that had been built to that point (connecting with 7 Muranowska). In the evenings Jurek would return to the ghetto with the Jewish workers.

During the period of the Jewish uprising, the men in Dr. Levy's group would go out at night through the ruins to Nalewki Street and attack the German guards. Jurek took an active part in these battles. At the end of May, when the position had become hopeless and ammunition and food were running out, the fighters decided to send Jurek to the Aryan side, in order to examine the possibilities of escape. After a protracted search for a way out through the tunnels and drains, Jurek eventually broke through by way of the Old City, and there made contact with some Polish smugglers. For a number of days they went in and out of the ghetto through the sewers, taking with them a Jewish family and returning the following day to the bunker of Dr. Levy's group at 11 Bonifraterska Street. One day, Jurek found only three people left there. The rest, among them Dr. Levy himself, had gone some hours earlier to the Aryan side in the company of a sewage worker. One of the last three went with Jurek. The others refused to leave.

Once out, Jurek found it difficult to organise some sort of existence for himself as he had no means of livelihood. In his wanderings through the town he met some cart drivers, who used to carry passengers between the Palace Square and the Gdanski Railway Station, and joined them. During one of his trips he met Wladek, a friend from before the war who now sold cigarettes on the trams, near Saski Park.

"Got a den?" asked Jurek.

Wladek didn't have one, but had heard that at the Polski Hotel, at 29 Dluga Street, there were some Jews waiting to go abroad. The two boys decided to visit the hotel and see if they could move out too.

In the hotel courtyard they found a crowd of several hundred Jews. It was an unbelievable sight, since Warsaw was officially *Judenrein*. Fires were dying out in the ruins of the ghetto, yet here were Jews, quite in the open, even without a Star of David on their clothes. Waiting for transport to neutral countries—as they believed—they boasted about their foreign passports bought with vast sums of money. Jurek and Wladek had no money for the 'hotel' or the 'trip' so they approached the ex-director of the place Mr. Guzik, who was there at the time, and asked him for help. Mr. Guzik advised them strongly against the journey, and gave each of the boys 500 zlotys.

"They don't want to help us because we have no money," complained the boys. They didn't know that the hotel was a trap. Many of those hiding on the Aryan side were taken in by this German ruse, volunteered for the trip abroad and were taken to extermination camps.

Soon afterwards, the two boys began selling cigarettes in the electric trains on the Otwock–Zyrardow line. They did fairly well, though they were often stopped by the railway police who, without realising their identity, confiscated their cigarettes. But shelter at night presented the greatest problem. Wladek met a Polish acquaintance from Otwock who allowed him to sleep in his rabbit hutch. Jurek remembered the Jewish cemetery on Okopowa Street. He used to work there once and knew the grounds. Finally, however, he chose the adjoining Catholic cemetery on Powazki. Somehow it seemed safer there. He discovered the tomb of a well-known merchant family Herse. The space inside the curve of the wall and behind the tomb itself seemed comfortable enough. At least it was always better than a damp cellar or ruins.

His first night there was terrifying. The trees seemed to have grown to frightening dimensions, the wind and leaves played an infernal music. The crosses standing on the graves looked like skeletons and the squeaking of bats chilled the blood in his veins. Shaking with fright and bathed in sweat, he realised fully that he was a victim of his own imagination, yet could not control his fear. With a determined effort he shut his eyes tightly and pulled his jacket over his head, but it did not help at all.

He could not possibly leave before morning, but he fully intended to run as soon as the curfew was lifted. At last daylight came, bringing peace and silence. Throughout the day he searched desperately for another shelter, but found nothing. When the curfew approached he again went to the cemetery. He returned there every night. In the morning, he would crawl out of his tomb, wash in a barrel of water, then, climbing over the wall, go into town. He would buy cigarettes and rush to catch the train where he worked. During the day he and Wladek used to work on their own, but at noon they would meet in the canteen to eat their lunches. After a while, Wladek joined him in the tomb, having been forced to leave his den when a neighbour recognised him.

One day, Wladek got up early and went to town; Jurek, tired out, slept on. He awoke to find people tidying the potted plants in his tomb. It must have been the family of the deceased. Without thinking, Jurek jumped out of his hole and ran towards the cemetery wall. His unexpected appearance frightened the relatives. Some of the women fainted, while others screamed, bringing out the caretaker. The den was 'blown'.

In the evening, unable to find another shelter, the two boys returned to the cemetery. They found another tomb, this time belonging to the Kuczynski family and, pushing away the heavy slab, crawled inside. Unfortunately the police, who had been notified by the family Jurek had disturbed, were watching the grounds. The boys emerged from their tomb next day, only to find policemen waiting among the trees. Seeing the trap, they bolted for the wall with the police at their heels, vaulted over the obstacle and jumped into a passing tram. From then on they could not return to the cemetery.

It was at this time that Jurek met our cigarette sellers. Wladek, after a few days' wandering, found a Polish friend who allowed him to sleep at his house and a few days later Jurek joined him there, and the two again took up cigarette-selling on the trains. Both boys regularly visited the Three Crosses Square to see how the others were managing, and during one of their visits learned that the children had been thrown out of their shelter. The cause of this disaster was little Bolus. He was peeing in the sink when Granny approached, looked closely, and yelled to her daughter:

"Mania, look, he's a Jew!"

In vain did Bolus try to deny it.

"You must all be Jews, then. Get out! Go!" she raged.

Nobody moved. The imbecile girl continued to play with her rabbit and paid no attention to the disturbance.

"Why are you screaming? Haven't we a right to live?" Bull asked.

"Get out! You lied to me, You should have told me at the start!"

"But Granny, we've nowhere to go," begged Teresa.

"I don't care. Get . . . !"

"We didn't mean to lie, but you'd never have let us in otherwise," explained Hoppy.

"Give her some money, maybe she'll quieten down," whispered Bull. Hoppy slipped 10 zlotys into the woman's hand. Turning her back, Granny examined the banknote.

"No, you must go. I can't keep you, someone may tell on me," she decided in a much softer voice.

"No one will tell, Granny. And if someone should say something, we'll finish him off," answered Hoppy, surprised by his own words.

The old woman looked astonished. "What do you mean?"

"There are Jews around with guns, who finish off all those who denounce us. Some even have machine guns!" he added slyly.

"My dear children, I can't, I'm scared, the district police have already asked about you."

"But it's late and we've nowhere to go for tonight," pleaded Teresa.

"You're too kind to chase us out now. It would be certain death," added Bull.

Granny considered for a moment. "All right. Stay for tonight, but tomorrow you must find another place."

The following night the children found shelter in a burnt-out house.

"Listen," said Bull, "I'll go once more to my teacher in Grochow. Maybe he'll let me sleep there."

When he arrived, Mr. Idzikowski looked embarrassed and showed no enthusiasm at the prospect. Only after Bull's earnest promise that he would leave early in the morning and return late at night did he relent and agree to take him in for a few nights.

Days passed, and the rains came. It was getting colder and sleep in the ruins became impossible. Once more the children decided to seek help from Granny.

"What do you want?" she snapped, as soon as she saw who it was.

"We've nowhere to sleep, please let us in for a few nights. The war will be over soon," begged Teresa.

"The Ruskis are near. When they come you'll get a reward," added Hoppy.

"I'm cold," complained little Bolus, blowing on his dirty hands, which were blue with cold.

"We'll give you five zlotys each," offered the practical Hoppy.

"Five zlotys, five zlotys," muttered the old woman. She turned to her daughter, who had been torturing the rabbit for an hour, vigorously trying to teach it to dance. "Mania! They're offering five zlotys each!"

"Who?" yelled the girl, frightened. But rapidly appraising the situation she ran to the ladder, looked suspiciously at the children and put out her hand.

Quickly the children pushed money into her palm and climbed the ladder.

"Go to bed, poor little mites, and be quiet so no one will hear you," said Granny, appeased, taking pity on the little 'lodgers' who would not let go of her skirts. That evening she prayed for a long time in front of the Blessed Virgin.

The following day, the children went as usual to Rozycki's bazaar. Bull waited for them at the entrance and the children told him about their new 'agreement'. In the afternoon Bolus joined them at the Square. He was panting and beaming with joy.

"What's happened?" asked Bull, surprised. At first Bolus couldn't catch his breath, but then he announced: "I've met one of ours under the bridge on Solec Street. He is from Saska Kepa. There are four of them. We are meeting tomorrow at noon."

Bull wanted to know more but Bolus could not add anything. After a short debate with Hoppy and Teresa, Bull decided to go to the rendezvous.

The Quartet from Saska Kepa

THE ACTION OF 1942 left the brothers Pawel and Zenek alone. For some time they succeeded in avoiding arrest, and finally decided to get out of the ghetto. Taking advantage of the usual confusion at the sentry post, they joined a group of workers and went out with them. They wandered around the town and earned their living singing in the courtyards. Every night they were faced with the problem of finding a shelter.

One night, while they crouched in the attic of a house at the corner of Saska Street and Washington Avenue, one of the tenants heard suspicious noises and notified the caretaker. He grabbed his torch and ran up to the hide-out, where he shone the torch right in the faces of the sleeping boys. They jumped to their feet, scared out of their wits.

"What are you doing here?"

"We are from Polus*, we missed the closing time," stammered Zenek.

"More likely you're after our clothes. We know your sort!"

The caretaker set about them with his stick. Without hesitation Zenek jumped over the railings and slid down the banister, followed by Pawel. They ran into the courtyard and reached the entrance, but the gates were shut. Followed

* Shelter for the homeless.

closely by the caretaker, they sprinted for the wooden fence and managed to climb over it, with Zenek pulling the weaker Pawel behind him.

"Thieves! You'll remember me!" screamed the caretaker, but the brothers ran and hid in the nearby cornfield where they sat, half-asleep, until the morning. They were hoping to get out unnoticed at dawn, but unfortunately a gang of road menders arrived. The boys suspected a trap. In their anxiety they saw a spy in everyone.

"We must separate," decided Pawel. "You run towards Saska Kepa and I'll go to Grochow. That way at least one of us will escape."

With one bound they jumped in amongst the corn and ran off in different directions. The workers simply stared after them, failing to understand what they were fleeing from. After a short time they met in the allotments between Saska Kepa and Grochow.

"No one followed me," said Zenek, trying to smile. His pride would not let him show how frightened he was.

"And me, when I looked round and saw nobody was after me, I thought they all ran after you," said Pawel.

"So we're both alive," joked Zenek. "Let's go, time's running out. We must get some money."

Coming to a courtyard, they went in, took up their position near a carpet beater and began to sing. From some of the windows people threw coins wrapped in paper.

"We've got a tenner," announced Zenek as they came out some time later. They looked into the next house and found two small boys who had been singing in that courtyard.

"How much did you make?" Zenek accosted them as they were leaving. After a short talk they 'sniffed' them out. One of the boys was Jankiel—Toothy—and the other was his nine-year-old brother.

"We're alone," said Toothy. "Mum and Dad died in hospital from typhus and our sister was taken to Treblinka. We sing in the courtyards. A Pole on Grochowska lets my brother sleep in his house and I climb over the railings into Skaryszewski Park and sleep between the chairs on the orchestra stand."

"We're alone too. We sleep in an attic. Last night we were caught by a caretaker. Look." Pawel showed his bruised hands and a lump on his forehead.

"There's another Jewish boy here on Saska Kepa," added Toothy. "Come and meet him."

At the end of Francuska Street a group of women worked on their allotments. A 13-year-old boy with typically Aryan features helped them carry buckets of water.

"Zbyszek!" called Toothy.

The boy left his buckets and jumped over the low fence to join his friends. His shirt and trousers were torn, showing the naked body underneath. He was barefoot and his face scratched as if he'd been in a fight.

"What do you want?" he asked sharply. "And who are they?" He pointed his finger disdainfully at Pawel and Zenek.

"They are 'ours'. We met today," said Toothy.

"In that case, let's shake."

"What street are you from?" asked Zenek.

"Ostrowska."

"When did you get out?"

"Oh, a long time ago. Everybody I was with died in 1941. I travel around, occasionally pinching something. I manage somehow. The day before yesterday some kids set on me so I punched one on the nose till he cried and then I tripped the other one and he ran. The third begged me not to beat him up, so I punched him too and he went away. No one jokes with me," boasted Zbyszek.

"Hey, by the way," he turned to Toothy, "a Polish woman told me some Jews were working on Grochowska Street."

"Let's go and see," suggested Pawel.

"Fine, only wait for me. I'll get some money from my old woman." Zbyszek ran back to the allotments to get his pay from the woman he was helping. She gave him five zlotys and he began to haggle.

"It's not enough! I've worked the whole day like a donkey . . . !"

The woman added a couple of zlotys and Zbyszek returned to his friends. Together they went to Grochowska Street where they found a group of Jews repairing the tram lines. The boys bought a few loaves of bread and took them to the men, who in exchange gave them various things—shirts, underpants and pillow-cases to sell. The workers returned each day to the ghetto and every now and again the boys went back with them to collect another load of old clothes for sale. In this way they continued for six months.

The third action of April 1943 caught Zenek and Toothy by surprise inside the ghetto. Zenek hid in an attic. There he was found by a German search party and sent to the Umschlagplatz. The boy managed to hide for three days in the building that stood on the Umschlagplatz and in the wood-stacks outside. He searched for some hole through which he could crawl out, but the whole place was closely guarded and in the end he went with the mass to the train hoping to escape on the way.

The train started towards Gdansk Station. Without hesitation Zenek broke through the barbed wire of the little window and jumped out. He turned head over heels, got up, grabbed a plank and lifted it on his back, pretending to be a labourer. Nearby, some Polish boys were busy stealing coal out of a railway truck. They saw Zenek and ran towards him. The boy was shaking with fear.

"What are you doing here? This is our spot! If you come once more we'll do you in!"

One of them kicked him, but after a brief scuffle they left him alone. Zenek, happy to be unrecognised, ran along the railway line towards Konarski Street. There he jumped into a tram going to Saska Kepa and returned to the others. Zbyszek and Pawel jumped up to meet him.

"How did you manage to get out? We thought you were a goner," said Zbyszek.

Zenek sat in the grass and told them about his escapade.

"And where's Toothy?"

"Still in the ghetto."

"He won't get out now. He'll go 'up the chimney' with the others," said Zbyszek quietly.

In the meantime Toothy had hidden in the porters' bunker at Mila Street, where he was found next day by a fighting unit from a neighbouring precinct, who had been forced out of their position by fire. A few days later the Germans set fire to the house in which the bunker was situated and all of them had to flee once more.

Under cover of night a group of crouching figures slipped out, to the accompaniment of machine-gun fire, among ruined and burning houses, across streets littered with feathers, clothes and a multiplicity of personal possessions. They reached a sewer and descended quickly, slamming the manhole cover above them. The whole of that day was spent sitting in the narrow tunnel, up to their knees in sewage, while above them the shooting continued unabated. They decided, like so many others before them, to get out to the Aryan side.

Toothy led the way holding a candle. For a long time they wandered, unable to find a way out. Whenever they did find an exit it turned out to be still in the ghetto. They realised this by the masses of feathers stuck to the gratings. Finally, suspecting that they were walking in a circle, they decided to signpost their way and stuck bits of paper to the walls.

On the third day of this terrible journey they met another group of five Jews, including two women, who were also searching for a way out of that maze. They joined forces, but still were unable to find an exit. Then on their fifth day underground they met two Poles working in the sewers, who for the price of 1,000 zlotys per person took them out to Lucka Street near the corner of Towarowa.

The manhole cover was lifted. Reeling, they followed one another out. The workers tried to stop Toothy as he had no money to pay them, but he managed to tear himself free and reach the street with the others. In the lavatory of a neighbouring house he found a newspaper with which he wiped his dirty face; then he cleared some of the mud off his clothes and ran as fast as his legs would carry him to his brother on Grochow. But the boy was not there. Toothy learned that, two days before, his brother had been taken away by a Polish policeman. No one had seen him since.

Exhausted, hungry and crying bitterly, Toothy dragged himself to Saska Kepa, where he fell asleep among the allotment huts. He was awakened by the morning coolness, rose, pumped up some water, undressed and washed thoroughly. After the filth and stench of the sewers, the cold water felt like a benediction. An hour later he was found by his friends.

"So you're alive? I thought you'd gone to the devil," Zbyszek greeted him.

Pawel and Zenek, horrified by these callous words, turned their back on Zbyszek and shared their breakfast bread with Toothy. Zbyszek was ashamed and repentant and pulled out a piece of sausage which he offered to the hungry boy—who swallowed the lot in a twinkling. Friends again, they set out together to find work on the allotments.

At that time Pawel had found a job on the allotments behind Skaryszewski Park. He had his permanent customers for whom he carried water and picked carrots. One day the caretaker, pitying the boy, offered him 100 zlotys per month to watch the allotments at night. This was a fantastic offer and Pawel accepted with joy. He now slept in a wooden hut which contained a camp bed with a blanket and a little table. The garden tools were stored in a cubby-hole.

"You'll be responsible for everything in here," warned the caretaker. Pawel nodded. "Remember, don't tell anyone that you are taking my place as caretaker. If one of the workers asks, say that I've gone out for a moment, and that I'll be back soon. Understand?" Pawel nodded again.

"What's the matter? Can't you talk?"

Blushing, Pawel replied quickly: "Yes, I understand." The caretaker looked at him suddenly as if he understood why the boy was afraid to talk. But in spite of his harsh words, there was sympathy and pity in his voice.

"Come back in the evening, but don't be late," he said.

Pawel returned to the boys at Saska Kepa. "Hey, fellows, I've got a den! Just like that!" he boasted, gesticulating triumphantly. "I'm watching some allotments at night. I've got a shed and 100 zlotys a month!"

The boys refused to believe it. "You can't fool us," chided Zbyszek.

"He's found some hole in the ground and calls it a shed," laughed Zenek.

But Pawel stuck to his guns. "If it's so good, maybe I can sleep there too?" said Zbyszek unexpectedly.

"I don't know how that would work out. The caretaker told me to come in the evening, but perhaps he'll change his mind. Today I'll see what the situation is. And tomorrow you can come," answered Pawel.

"You see how I put him in his place? He's already withdrawn like a crab." jeered Zbyszek.

"Bluffer," dismissed Toothy.

The children scattered. Pawel ran to the caretaker at the allotments.

"Ah! You're here nice and early. Here are the keys. See that everything goes O.K.," he said as he left.

Pawel wandered around the allotments pulling up carrots and scraping them with his pen-knife. Afterwards he lay down full-length on the couch. It was a long time since he had been able to sleep so comfortably. Early in the morning the caretaker came, knocked several times, and got no answer. Pawel, worn out, was sleeping the sleep of the just. The caretaker became annoyed and began to bang on the door. At this, Pawel woke up in a panic. The caretaker entered and glanced all around him, looking into the cupboard until he was satisfied that everything was in its place.

"How've you slept, little 'un?" he asked the boy.

"Well," smiled Pawel, still half asleep.

"Wash your face. There's a bucket of water over there. Today you will come a bit earlier," said the caretaker. "And take out the work tools from the hut."

Pawel washed himself and ran to Saska Kepa to the boys. "Well, how's the 'job'?" sneered Zbyszek.

They went together to the allotments to help the women. Zbyszek and Pawel carried water for their plants and vegetables, Zenek dug the beds and Toothy repaired fences. At noon one of the women Mrs. Leokadia Pycek, the caretaker at No. 3 Radziwillowska Street—invited them home for lunch and then they returned together to work. In the evening Pawel went to his shed. He cleaned the tools and stored them in the cubby-hole. When darkness fell. Zbyszek stole through the fence and stood for a moment listening. Everything was quiet. He ran to the shed and knocked three times.

"What a swell place," he cried, looking round.

"You see, I wasn't lying," said Pawel, pleased. From then on, Zbyszek came every night.

One afternoon the two boys went to Grochowska Street to visit a shoemaker whom Pawel knew since before the war. They were having tea together when suddenly a *Volksdeutsch-bahnschutz* (railway policeman) walked in. The shoemaker's apprentice whispered in his ear that the visitors were Jews, and the policeman called the two boys out in the street.

"Come on, admit it," he encouraged them. "I won't harm you. I had a Jewess in my house, you know, and I sent her out to work on a farm. I can send you too, you'll be safe there."

The two boys, frightened, denied everything.

"Don't be so scared, nothing will happen to you. Come home with me, we'll have something to eat," coaxed the Volksdeutsch gently. The boys, gaining confidence, followed him to his house at 36 Targowa Street. The man's wife was in bed, so the Volksdeutch decided to go directly to a farmer in Wlochy. Together, they boarded a tram, reached Central Station and entered the hall. But instead of going to the platforms, the man took them straight to the railway police. By the time the boys realised that they were trapped it was too late to escape. The Volksdeutsch pushed them inside.

"Das sind zwei Juden," he reported to the paunchy station commandant.

The boys stood speechless, convinced that their last hour had struck.

"Mr. Commandant" explained Pawel in a trembling voice, "*me nix Jude.*" He began a Christian prayer, known more or less to all these Jewish children.

Zbyszek stood silently. His Aryan face spoke for itself. The commandant ordered Pawel to say *Brot* (for knowledge of German aroused suspicion). The boy said *'Prot'*. This apparently satisfied the German, or perhaps he was not keen to exterminate two Jewish children discovered by a local zealot.

"Get out of here," he yelled suddenly; and the boys, saved by a miracle, jumped for the door. They ran as fast as their legs would carry them, turning to see that no one was following, their hearts pounding like hammers, until, drenched with sweat, they reached Saska Kepa, where they fell on the grass, panting. Nervously, they looked around for their friends.

"They must have gone for the night," decided Zbyszek.

"Hey, I've got to go to my shed," remembered Pawel. He jumped up, brushed down his clothes, wiped his face, smoothed his hair and sped towards the park, shouting to Zbyszek to follow him soon.

The Orphanage in Wolska Street

ZENEK AND TOOTHY had difficulty finding a place to sleep, but eventually came upon an attic in Saska Kepa.

"Here, this seems all right." Zenek pointed to a corner divided from the rest of the attic by two leaning planks. They lay close to each other to keep warm.

Going down the stairs the next morning they ran into the caretaker.

"What are you doing here?" he asked suspiciously. "You've been thieving!"

"No, no, sir, we never, we only slept here," explained Zenek, suddenly losing confidence and pulling nervously at his trousers.

The caretaker grabbed hold of their collars and led them outside. The boys were trying to free themselves when they were suddenly confronted by a policeman.

"They are thieves, I caught them in the attic," cried the caretaker.

"Please constable, we haven't stolen anything, please let us go!"

"You didn't steal anything? Why, I can read it in your eyes, you're a thief!" The policeman slapped Zenek's face.

"Why are you hitting me? Why?"

"You're coming to the police station. We'll soon see who you are!"

He grabbed the boys by their sleeves and in a few moments they were at the station. The constable went in to talk to the commandant, leaving the boys in the waiting room.

"This time it's the end for us," muttered Toothy, when the office door opened again.

"Come here, little angels," cried the fat sergeant from behind his desk. Toothy followed Zenek inside.

"What's your name?"

"Zenon Borkowski."

"How old are you?"

"Twelve."

"Where do you live?"

"In Pludy."

"Ah, I see you've run away from home. Is that it?"

"Yes, Dad beat me so I ran away," lied Zenek, catching on quickly.

"Why?"

"Because we'd been smoking," offered Toothy.

"And what did you pinch from that attic? Go on, let's have it, I won't hurt you."

"We didn't steal anything, we only slept there," explained Toothy.

"Wait outside," ordered the policeman finally, picking up the telephone.

"I've got two young customers for you. Do you have room for them?" he asked. "Yes? Very well, I'm sending them over."

The boys exchanged a glance. Where to?

"Come on, innocents," called a constable.

"But where to, sir, why? We haven't taken anything," repeated Toothy stubbornly.

"Oh, stop explaining. Come on, you only die once," interrupted Zenek.

They went out. The policeman tied their hands with a piece of string and led them towards the centre of Warsaw.

"I've got a penknife. If he's taking us to Ujazdowskie

Avenue, which means the Gestapo, I'll cut the string and we can run for it in opposite directions," whispered Toothy.

They approached Nowy Swiat.

"If we turn here, it means trouble," muttered Toothy, squinting to his left.

"Please, sir," Zenek touched the policeman's hand, "do we turn here?"

"No, straight on."

The boys cheered up immediately. They followed along Jerozolimskie Avenue and turned at Zelazna Street. On reaching Wolska they stopped at the corner of Karolkowa Street. Toothy looked up at the four-storey house which still bore the sign 'Jewish Old People's Home'. They went inside. It was a Christian orphanage now. In the large courtyard boys and girls played with a ball. Nearby a group of younger children made sandcastles in some sand. Seeing the newcomers the boys left their games and ran towards them.

"New boys!"

They pressed around in a tight circle, pushing, shoving and asking questions.

"You push me again and I'll show you!" cried Zenek.

"Look at him, look at him, he's still showing off!" laughed the others, pointing to their hands which were still tied. But when the policeman cut the string, the children scattered prudently and kept their distance.

An hour later, Zenek and Toothy emerged from the bathroom wearing clean shirts under their torn and dirty jackets and soon joined in the games, forgetting everything else. The dinner bell interrupted the fun. They sat down at a table and after a short prayer ate their soup. Toothy finished his quickly and got up but was told by one of the nuns that there was meat to follow. Meat? The boy looked surprised. After their meal, everybody got up and went out to the courtyard again. Zenek could hardly move and patted his full stomach with glee.

"Well, how do you like it?" asked Toothy.

"Not bad, not bad, we can't complain," answered Zenek.

Some of the boys sat at small tables, doing their lessons. Zenek and Toothy wandered around until a nun appeared bringing paper and pencils.

"Write down your life history."

"What can we write?" they asked one another.

"Let's write a letter to the boys," Zenek agreed.

"We are in a children's home on Wolska Street," they wrote. "We've got everything we need. We play ball. Pity you are not here." Toothy folded the page and addressed it to his aunt, Mrs. Lodzia on Saska Kepa, adding, "for Pawel and Zbyszek." They ran to the fence where they saw a street sweeper on the other side.

"Please, sir, send this to my aunt on Saska Kepa. She doesn't know where I am. Here are five zlotys for you," said Zenek.

The man took their letter, promising to send it.

"Look out, here comes the old woman," warned Toothy, and they sat down again.

"How is it going?" asked the nun.

"Not ready yet," they answered, bending down over their pieces of paper.

"How on earth do we begin?" sighed Zenek.

"We'll see who can lie better," challenged Toothy. He began to write, speaking the words aloud. " 'My name is Jan Jankowski. I was born in the village . . .' what village?" he wondered.

"Write down your story and don't interrupt," Zenek muttered crossly.

Toothy went on: " 'I was born in the village of Wolka near . . .' " he meditated for a few seconds . . . " ' near Malkinia.' There must be a Wolka somewhere there. 'That was in . . .' Hey, is it better to be younger or older?' " he asked Zenek again.

"I don't know, younger probably . . ."

"Well then. 'That was in 1933. . . . When I was seven I went to school and I helped father on the farm. In 1941 father was killed by . . . bandits and mother was deported to Germany. I was left alone.' I've finished. I'm signing it."

"So fast?" asked Zenek.

"How much more do you want? In any case I can't tell the truth. If I did their hair would stand on end."

"I am giving them a whole spiel," boasted Zenek.

"Show me!"

"No, not till I finish."

Toothy snatched the paper from his hand and Zenek ran after him.

"Give it back!"

"When I've read it!"

Zenek, seeing he could never catch him, sat down. Toothy read quietly:

'My name is Zenon Borkowski. My father works as a wheelwright on an estate. My mother works in the house. I have two brothers and a younger sister and an 89-year-old grandmother. I was born in 1931 in Pludy, near Warsaw. I went to school when I was seven. My elder brother helped me with my school work. In 1939 a shell destroyed our house. We had to build it again. I helped too. Now we have a very nice house . . .'

"You are a fine story teller," laughed Toothy. "Pity you didn't mention your great-grandmother."

Zenek sang softly: "You've got to have an Aryan grandmother, 'cause without her, you're lost, my brother."

They both laughed.

Days passed. The boys played games, attended lessons and made some progress in their education. Their only worry was the suspicious glances of one of the teachers, although they avoided the communal bath as best they could. However, after a month, in spite of all their efforts, suspicion of their true origins became very real. At first it took the form of malicious talk and the occasional small unpleasantness. The teacher who was praising their school work added: "You have . . . commercial talent". Later still the older children began calling them Jews. When the sister on duty assigned them some heavy chores, the boys saw in it—perhaps unjustly—a sign of persecution. Finally they were called for a medical examination.

"We've got to run," Toothy decided. "They all know."

"Boys, the doctor is waiting," called a nun.

"We're coming, sister."

They entered the building, but instead of turning left to the surgery, they turned right towards the gate. Quickly, they ran down the corridor, pushed open the gate and jumped for the street.

"Boys, where are you off to?" called the porter.

"Back in a minute!" they answered and disappeared into the crowded street.

They returned to Saska Kepa. Pawel was digging a bed on the allotment, while Zbyszek, sitting on a tree stump, whistled a song.

"Hey, look! Here come the institution kids!" He yelled. "Well, how was it? Are the fat years over?"

"Nothing to complain about," replied Toothy.

"Another orphanage like that won't hurt," added Zenek.

Wladek, 1944

Bull, leader of the gang, 1944

Toothy (right) with his younger brother, 1943

Zbyszek (left) and Burek. The caption reads, "Greetings from Warsaw, 1944"

Little Stasiek, 1944

*Stefcia, photographed
during the 1944 Uprising*

Romek (left) and Stasiek-from-Praga, 1944

Frenchy, 1944

The Amchu

ONE EVENING IN SEPTEMBER 1943 Pawel, Zbyszek and Zenek
were hanging around in the field between the Skaryszewski
Park and Grochowska Street. Suddenly Zenek whispered:
"Look, look, there . . . something's moving!" and pointed to a
hole in the ground.

"It's a man. He's coming out," added Pawel.

"Must be a vagabond, but he walks like a Jew," said
Zbyszek.

The mysterious figure straightened up and walked away
towards Washington Avenue.

"Who can it be?" wondered Pawel.

"Come on, let's see," Zbyszek pulled the resisting Zenek.
"What are you afraid of? Cowards!" Zenek and Pawel moved
on. Slowly, bent double, they crawled towards the place from
which the stranger had emerged.

"Maybe there's another one down there," warned Pawel.

Zbyszek disregarded his words and crept nearer. A few
yards before the hole they crouched down and listened. Nothing
stirred. They approached nearer. A wooden plank partly
covered with moss protruded from the earth. They pushed it
aside and saw a large hole, lined with straw. There was a
hunk of bread and a glass jar in one corner. The boys broke
into an excited babble.

100

"Someone is hiding here . . ."

"Perhaps he's a Jew . . . "

"Or from the Resistance . . ."

"Must be a Jew, the bread gives him away." Pawel stuck to his opinion.

"Don't talk nonsense, they'd have found him long ago. . . ."

"I'm telling you it's a Jew!"

"We'll see. I'll catch him." Zbyszek ended their argument.

"Just cover the hole exactly as it was before," advised Zenek.

Pawel covered the plank with moss. The boys retreated to a nearby copse and from there watched the field. Half an hour passed by and no one appeared. It began to rain.

"Lets go, we'll catch him tomorrow," proposed Zbyszek.

They left. Pawel and Zbyszek went back to their shed on the allotment, Zenek, to Mrs. Lodzia where Toothy was already waiting. Zenek told them about the discovery. "Someone lives in there. He is even worse off than we are."

Mrs. Lodzia, moved by the story, took pity on the boys. She offered to let them sleep in her cellar. "Only be careful no one sees you."

The following evening Pawel, Zbyszek and Zenek again waited in the copse for the unknown man. And again as soon as darkness fell, someone began crawling out from the earth. The boys stared. The man rose, looked around and began walking away. The boys followed.

"Let's go faster so we can pass him and take a good look," proposed Zenek.

"No. We'll run to Washington Avenue and wait under the street lamp. He must pass that way," decided Zbyszek, and all three sprinted across the field.

The mysterious stranger passed the allotment fence, reached Washington Avenue and turned towards Saska Kepa. He walked fast, anxiously looking around. Seeing the boys under the street lamp he pulled out a handkerchief and pretended to blow his nose so that he covered his face.

Pawel sat stooping and Zenek glanced up surreptitiously; only Zbyszek looked the man straight in the face. In the light

of the lamp he could see clearly the typically Semitic features.
He got up and approached him.

"Excuse me please, what time is it?"

"I don't know."

The man was walking fast. It seemed that he was restraining himself from running.

"Don't be afraid, we're friends," said Zbyszek.

The man stopped for a moment as if out of breath.

"Don't go that way, there are gendarmes there," warned Zenek and Pawel.

"So what, I live here, on Saska Kepa, and I am going home."

Zenek looked around. No one was in sight.

"Ich bin ein Yid," he whispered.

The man stopped dead in his tracks. He stared at Zenek, glanced at Pawel and Zbyszek, then again at Zenek. The boy nodded.

"I am *amchu* too," said Pawel.

"Me too," added Zbyszek.

The man, looking at Zbyszek's Aryan face, refused to believe it. "He, a Jew?" he asked incredulously. The boys nodded.

"We go round begging, we sleep in attics and cellars, we manage somehow," they began. "We hold on to the wind, just so we don't give up the bona*," interrupted Zbyszek. A faint smile appeared on the man's face. This expression from the ghetto dispersed his last doubts. But after a moment his face grew sad again.

"Come on, it's dangerous to stop here," he told the boys and they turned into a side street. The stranger told them of his experiences, how he used to live in Nowolipie Street and lost his entire family.† Now he had found his little hole where

---

* Bread coupons, in the language of the ghetto. 'To give up the bona' meant 'to die'.

† The man was a fighter from the ghetto—Aleksander Celnikier. On the 29th of April 1943 he and several others left the ghetto through sewers. The Polish Resistance took them to the forest where they joined the partisans. After two months of fighting the Germans broke up the unit, and many of the partisans were killed. Celnikier, after many dramatic experiences, managed to reach Warsaw.

he sat all day long, coming out only at night to search for food. Looking closely, they realised that he was still quite young, though unshaven and terribly thin.

"I don't know what's going to happen. I'll starve to death. A friend of mine, a Baptist, brings me bread sometimes, but winter is coming. . . ."

"We'll help you," chorused the boys and Zenek pulled five zlotys from his pocket.

"We'll ask Mrs. Lodzia for some soup. She won't refuse," added Zbyszek.

"Someone is coming," whispered Zenek and the group broke up quickly.

"Where will we meet?" asked the man.

"In the copse tomorrow at eight, when it gets dark!" Zenek called softly. And off they went, all in different directions.

The following evening the boys begged Mrs. Lodzia for a billycan of hot soup and then went to meet him at the appointed place. It was dark. The man was already waiting.

"My dear boys!" he cried at their approach. "I thought you weren't coming, that you'd forgotten!"

"We forget? You doubted our word?' Zbyszek was almost offended. But the man paid no attention to their words. His mind was preoccupied with something else.

"What have you got there?" he asked, his eyes riveted to the steam rising from the can. With trembling hands he raised it to his mouth and in one gulp swallowed the whole lot.

"Thank you, thank you," he repeated, wiping his lips and breathing heavily. "It's months since I've eaten anything hot! Now, come with me; I'll show you my den."

"No, no thank you. We've got to go now; we'll be back tomorrow," said the boys.

They split up. Zenek went to Saska Kepa, and Pawel and Zbyszek to their hut.

"Did you see how that 'cat' guzzled his soup?" asked Zbyszek.

"Hardly surprising, considering how hungry he was," replied Pawel. "But he's a fine man, he's an 'Amchu'."

From then on the children brought soup and bread to 'the Amchu' every day.

September was ending. The owners of the allotments dismantled the little tool-shed and Pawel and Zbyszek were again homeless and without a job. They began hunting around and came to Skaryszewski Park.

"Look, this could be a fine den," Pawel pointed to a place under the steps.

"Let's do some work on it."

Pawel ran to Washington Avenue and brought some old bricks. Zbyszek dragged in a bundle of straw, stolen from a nearby house. They stuffed the straw under the stairs, making a sort of a lair, then spread some of it out as a kind of bed and placed on it two sacks, taken surreptitiously by Zbyszek from a nearby cellar. Then they stacked the bricks on one side of the hole to form a wind-break. The other side served as an entrance. The den was ready and all the boys had to do was push their way in through the narrow entrance and lie down to sleep. Unfortunately the nights were cold and soon after Pawel caught a chill in his bladder and soaked the straw. Next morning, cold and stiff, they walked to Saska Kepa. There they met Zenek and Toothy, who still slept in the cellar of the house where Mrs. Lodzia was a caretaker. In the evening they brought soup for the Amchu and returned to their hide-out.

"Zbyszek, we ought to change the straw, it's wet," said Pawel.

"Go and find some then, I'm not going to pinch it for you," replied Zbyszek, alluding to the fact that it was Pawel's fault the straw was wet.

"Look at him, so overworked . . . ! "

"Oh, all right, throw the straw out into the lake and we'll look for some more together," Zbyszek agreed.

But this time it was not as easy as on the first day. A fiercely growling dog met them at the wooden fence at the house the straw was taken from before, and Pawel instinctively drew back.

"What's the matter? You're not afraid of the Germans but you run from a dog?" mocked Zbyszek.

They climbed over the fence, only to find their access to the straw barred. The dog, tied on a long chain, barked furiously. Zbyszek made a gesture as if throwing a stone and the animal retreated.

"Don't be frightened, we're scared too! What's he barking for? He's got somewhere to sleep, and he's got a kennel, yet he's too mean to let us have a bundle of straw."

But the dog showed no understanding of their basic needs. Any moment now and his barking would bring someone to investigate the commotion.

"Shut your noise, it won't help you!"

Pawel ran towards the house. The dog followed. Then Zbyszek ran in, grabbed a bundle of straw, and fled the other way.

New Mates (The Union)

ONE DAY, IN OCTOBER 1943, Toothy was walking down Solec Street when he noticed a small boy whose face seemed familiar. He looked straight into his eyes and the child, frightened, turned quickly into a side street. Toothy ran after him.

"Hey there, don't you know me? Remember how we climbed over the wall together?" he called, seeing that there was no one around.

The boy stopped. "What wall?"

Toothy laughed and patted him on the back. "We're both the same, don't worry. There are a few of us here. We live on our wits, our main aim is not to give up the bona."

"So do we. We sell cigarettes," boasted the child. It was Bolus.

"How can we meet the others?" asked Toothy.

"I don't know, I'll ask Bull."

" 'Bull'?"

"He's the eldest."

"Tell him to come tomorrow at noon, under the bridge. We'll be waiting. Don't forget!"

"All right, I won't forget. I'll tell him," Bolus assured him, running as fast as he could towards Three Crosses Square.

Toothy watched the boy disappear and blew on his palms for luck; then he himself sprinted towards Saska Kepa. He could hardly wait to tell his friends the sensational news. Out

of breath and streaming with sweat he reached the allotments.
"I've got news!" he cried as soon as he was in earshot.
The boys surrounded him in a circle.
"What's happened?"
"What's the news?"
"I've met one of our boys," spluttered Toothy. "I've made a date for tomorrow under the bridge!"
"We'll all go!" they decided.
And that was the moment, which will be remembered from an earlier chapter, when Bolus arrived breathless and excited at Three Crosses Square to announce the news of *his* discovery.
Next day the four boys from Saska Kepa marched towards Solec Street. It was cold. Zbyszek walked fast, rubbing his hands to keep warm. Pawel hurried them on, afraid they would be late. Quickly they ran down the steps of the bridge and waited. Mindful of the constant danger, Zbyszek strolled to and fro under the bridge, carefully scrutinising each passer-by. There were a few people waiting at the tram stop. From the nearby hospital came the sound of a German radio. A street seller loudly praised her apples.
"Me and Toothy will wait near the steps," ordered Pawel. "Zbyszek, you go behind the bridge, near the hospital; Zenek on the other side. If you see something, whistle."
Zbyszek went to his post and leaned against the wall, observing the street. On the other side of the bridge Zenek played with some pebbles to avoid attention. They did not have to wait long, for Bull and Bolus arrived after a few minutes, approaching Pawel and Toothy first. Zenek and Zbyszek hurried to join them, drawn on by curiosity, but Pawel quickly sent them back to their posts.
"What do you do? Where do you live?" asked Bull, trying not to attract attention.
"We live, we live . . ." stammered Pawel, embarrassed. "We don't live anywhere, we sleep in the ruins and pass the days on Saska Kepa."
"And what do you do? How many of you are there?" Toothy couldn't contain his curiosity.

"We . . ." began Bull. He had no time to continue. Zbyszek's whistle warned them of danger. Two gendarmes were approaching. Instantly the boys scattered in all directions. When the Germans had gone they met again.

Pawel told Bull how they existed, working on the allotments and being paid with food or money. "We have a Polish woman, Mrs. Lodzia. She lets us in when it's raining. Toothy and Zenek sleep in her cellar and Zbyszek and I sleep wherever we can, in attics, on the allotments, in the ruins or under the stairs. We go round like tramps. And winter is coming . . ." he ended with a sigh.

"Maybe the war will end before the frosts set in; in the meantime we'll all go to Granny's," Bull announced calmly. Pawel looked surprised. "She's an old woman who lets us sleep in her room. She'll let you too."

"Us too?" the boys looked incredulously at Bull.

"Yes, of course she will let you in. We won't leave you on the street. There were five of us till today, so now we'll be nine."

The boys listened unbelievingly. Their eyes shone with happiness. Bull continued: "We'll go to Three Crosses Square so you can meet the band. I'll explain everything and teach you what to do. Have you got a few zlotys for cigarettes?"

"Yes, we have," cried Zenek.

"Fine, we'll buy a few *Swojaks* and then, if all goes well, you'll buy some real ones and you're in business."

They approached the Square. "Now, let's separate," Bull said. "Two together at the most. Don't go near ours—I'll point them out as we go past. We'll talk in the evening at Granny's."

Bull and Pawel went on first, followed by Zenek and Zbyszek a few yards behind. Toothy and Bolus brought up the rear.

"See there, under that wall, that boy with cigarettes? He may be ours," remarked Zenek.

"I'll go and look him straight in the eye; if he's scared he's ours," said Zbyszek, taking a few steps in that direction. Zenek jumped and pulled him back.

"Are you crazy? You want to give him away?" he whispered furiously.

They went on. Near the Church of St. Alexander stood Hoppy with a packet of cigarettes. Seeing Bull with a strange boy, he called out loudly: "Swojaks, Swojaks, single and in packets!" to attract their attention. Bull nodded slightly to show he had noticed.

"He's ours, we call him Hoppy," he informed Pawel.

"Heavens, what's going on here? It's the whole of Nalewki*," whispered Zbyszek in astonishment.

"Give me 10 zlotys each, for cigarettes. I'll buy them for you," Bull offered turning to Toothy.

"I haven't got that much," said the boy, embarrassed.

"Give me what you've got, then, I'll lend you the rest." Toothy took a few zlotys from his pocket.

"And take mine too." Bolus handed over the two zlotys he'd earned that day. Then he approached each of the newcomers asking in whispers if they were from Nowolipie, his home street.

However, the question upset Zbyszek who immediately snapped bitterly: "What? Get away from me, or I'll kick you!"

The little one took several steps back, gave Zbyszek a sideways glance and ran for it. He almost collided with Bull and began complaining to him in a weeping voice.

"He wants to beat me," pointing to Zbyszek, who was still standing by the church. Bull burst out laughing.

An hour later, the new boys were walking round the Square with packets of cigarettes, shyly crying their wares. They were not very successful at first, uncertain in their movements, not knowing how to approach a customer. The Polish boys looked at them disdainfully, and maliciously stole their customers at the last moment just before the bargain was concluded, as when a Polish boy ran past hissing: "Coppers!" just as a passerby was choosing his cigarettes from Toothy.

Toothy vanished and his place was immediately taken by two other boys who took the business from him.

"Don't worry," Bull consoled him. "Rome wasn't built in a day." At three o'clock the boys went to the canteen on Zorawia

* Formerly the principal street in the Jewish quarter.

109

Street. "What, there are more of you again? Soon we won't have enough soup to feed everybody!" exclaimed the cook. But she did not refuse another helping, which Pawel and Zbyszek poured into a billy-can for the Amchu.

"Take me with you this time," pleaded Bolus. "I want to see this grown-up Jew—he might be from my family."

In the evening they went to Saska Kepa to meet the 'grown-up Jew'. They passed the copse and looked around to see if they were being followed; seeing no one they ran to the hide-out. The Amchu grabbed the billy-can silently and drank the contents in one gulp. He breathed deeply and smiled as if to thank the boys for their help. Then he looked suspiciously at the small stranger, Bolus, but the latter put out a hand to greet him. They stared at each other.

The oppressive silence was broken by the boy's words: "I have a present for you."

The Amchu looked surprised. He had no idea what the boy meant. The word 'present' was quite strange to him now.

Quickly, Bolus pulled a loaf of bread and a packet of cigarettes from his dirty fur coat. The Amchu, astonished, could find no words to thank him. He wanted to embrace the child, to kiss him, but an unexplained impulse paralysed his arms. For the first time in many months he felt tears gathering in his eyes and he felt even smaller, even more helpless than Bolus.

Pawel and Zbyszek were equally surprised. They had not suspected that Bolus was hiding something in his clothes. After saying good-bye to the man the three boys returned to Three Crosses Square to work. They had done well that day and now they bought a cake for each member of the band to celebrate. It was a long time since they had been so happy.

"If only it was always like this," sighed Toothy.

"Look, it's going to rain," Pawel pointed to the cloudy sky. This brought them back to reality. "What are we going to do tonight?"

"So, we'll get soaked. . . . You won't die, water doesn't bite," joked Zbyszek.

At that moment they were joined by Bull. "What's the matter? Are you worried about tonight? We'll all go to Granny's."

They walked towards Krucza Street, Bull and Zenek leading the way, and when they reached Granny's house the daughter was first to greet them.

"For heaven's sake, how many of you are there?"

"Never mind, we'll give you money for medicine," Bull assured her.

The boys pulled out a zloty each, pushed it into her hand and one after the other slipped inside the room. As usual, money softened her resistance. She dragged the ladder up to the loft.

"Up you go, my little angels."

In a moment they were upstairs. A few minutes later Granny entered, and seeing the unexpected crowd began screaming. "You haven't paid yet and you're up there already? Get down, all of you!"

"Shush, Granny—in a minute," assured Bull. He collected the money and took it down to the old woman, who counted it and pushed the lot inside her clothes.

"Well, you see, everything is all right, we are honest," commented Hoppy from the loft.

"Keep quiet now and don't muck up the floor, or I'll throw the lot of you out!" Granny delivered her customary warning as she lay down among the rags of her divan.

Soon the group increased again. One day, as Bull was walking with Hoppy among the stalls of Rozycki's bazaar, he felt someone pushing him. He started with fright. Another push, this time stronger. Prepared for the worst, Bull turned and immediately his fear gave way to surprise. Before him stood Conky—who, it will be remembered, had left Warsaw to work on a farm, out of the reach of the shmalzers. He was dirty, clad in a ragged Russian coat and huge, torn peasant's boots.

"Where have you been all this time?" Bull and Hoppy

asked simultaneously. The three of them entered a nearby house and Conky related his adventures.

"I worked at a farm from dawn till night, but at least I had somewhere to sleep. In the end though, they began to suspect me. The whole village was talking, so I had to run. I've been in Warsaw a few days now—I sleep in the bushes on the riverside," he ended.

"Why didn't you look for us?" asked Hoppy.

"Where was I to look? I went to Mrs. Kalot, but she didn't know where you were. I thought you were all gone."

"We're not so stupid," announced Bull happily. Then he and Hoppy took Conky to the steam bath in Gigant, where his clothes were deloused. (The bath in fact was in a doss house in Jagiellonska Street.) Bull gave him a shirt, Hoppy a scarf and they led him, freshly dressed, to the Three Crosses Square. There Bull provided him with cigarettes and installed the newcomer on the corner of Nowy Swiat, near a German restaurant called 'Vier Jahreszeiten'. They gave him a quick explanation of what to do and Conky started in business. He felt newly born. He was earning money, he had friends and he had a roof over his head. He kept close to Bull and gradually became his 'lieutenant'.

It was about this time that Bull met Kazik, the French boy who had tried to escape with him from the train taking captured ghetto fighters to Poniatow, and who had been recaptured by the Germans—only to escape subsequently from the camp itself. The boys nicknamed him Frenchy.

Later on Conky recognised another Jewish boy loitering barefoot in the streets and brought him to the Square. They collected some money to buy him a pair of wooden clogs, and nicknamed him 'the Peasant' because he had worked for many months on a farm. He had learned to speak like a peasant and was dressed accordingly. The nickname stuck to him for good, long after he had lost his peasant ways.

Both newcomers were lent some money to buy cigarettes, but from then on they were on their own, given their own stands—Frenchy on Prus Street, at the corner of Three Crosses

Square near the Hungarian barracks, the Peasant on Konopnicka Street in front of the SS-occupied Y.M.C.A.

Great was their astonishment when one day they noticed yet another small boy, poorly dressed, wandering aimlessly through the Square. His looks left them in no doubt as to his identity and quickly they found a common language.

This newcomer was another Stasiek, "little" Stasiek (to distinguish from the 17-year-old who had been with the cigarette sellers for some time). He was helpless and, as his face attracted suspicion, he was not given anything to sell but was allowed only to keep the stock. Even so, some of the boys were unhappy about his presence on the Square. Bull tried to convince them that they could not drive the child away, but on the contrary had to help him. To the new one's namesake, Mosze-Stasiek, the spokesman for those who were against the boy, Bull said severely: "What are you afraid of? He's no worse than you are."

The cigarette business was developing satisfactorily. The Jewish boys were gaining experience. Bull, too, although often busy with other matters, managed to do well.

Near the Soldatenheim a few boys, Polish and Jewish, surrounded a German soldier. Each wanted to sell his cigarettes. They shoved and jostled, pushing their packets under the soldier's nose, but he pushed them back disdainfully. He wanted neither 'Mewy' nor the German 'Juno', but was searching for something better.

"What about some filtertips?" proposed a Pole.

"I've got American! American!" cried Bull.

The German examined them carefully. "Where did you get these?"

"From aerial drops!" laughed a Pole at his side.

The soldier took the cigarettes and paid up. But this competition was not limited to the Poles. The boys quarreled and fought among themselves, not only because of the money involved, but so as to be able to boast to the rest of the band. They were capable of 'tripping' even their closest friends; they bargained, haggled and undersold each other eagerly.

113

Trouble with Bolus

ONE DAY A LARGE contingent of Hungarians from the Eastern Front came to the barracks at the corner of Prus Street and Three Crosses Square, and immediately the boys began making plans to establish contact with them.

"We could make a lot of money out of them," argued Bull.

"But how can one talk to them?" a Polish boy standing nearby asked in a loud voice.

Toothy ran to the nearest paper shop, bought some picture postcards of Warsaw and went over to the Hungarians. Talking in sign language, he managed to acquire in the next few minutes several packets of Hungarian and German cigarettes and a tin of meat. He sold all these immediately for a good price in the nearby street and then returned to the Square. Contact had been established.

The boys felt a strange sympathy for the Hungarians as they started trading with them. The soldiers on their part often gave the children presents from their own stores. Belts, billy-cans, bandages and the like all found their way into the boys' hands—the Hungarians explaining in broken German that they "had had enough of that war". The Hungarian barracks became a meeting point for the cigarette sellers who bought many things very cheaply. Among the sellers was Bolus who

114

came every few hours to help his elders. He carried their cigarettes, brought picture postcards and letter paper, held the money they earned and watched out for police or gendarmes.

At times, in the process of buying cigarettes, preserves, or other things arguments, quarrels and even fights would break out amongst the Jewish boys. In these problems and quarrels, Bull was the final arbiter. And generally he would try to see that friction of this kind did not arise with Polish boys, who also traded in the Square.

The trade with the Hungarians brought the boys a good income, which they shared out between themselves. With the money they would buy a good meal. Their health improved and their pale faces began to show some colour. They paid more attention to cleanliness, so difficult in the circumstances, and almost every week went together to the baths in Gigant, where they also cleaned and deloused their clothes. They played at being V.I.P.'s by giving a large tip to the bath attendant, so that he would not let anyone else in. In fact this was a necessary safety precaution against recognition. They took their dinners at the R.G.O. and in the evening went to their various dens, most of them sleeping at Granny's on Krucza Street.

Those evenings at Granny's turned into regular conferences. It was the only place where they could talk freely about the day's events and their successes or problems, where they could discuss new ways of earning money and make important decisions.

Their shrewdness in dealing with the Hungarians inspired jealousy and suspicion in the Poles. They have 'Jewish heads,' said the Polish boys, and often picked on the younger boys, who were immediately defended by their elders.

Little Bolus, the Benjamin of the group, was the most frequent target for attack. Since the disappearance of his little girl friend, he had given up singing in the trams and now spent his days on the Square. The tram conductors and the caretakers of nearby houses knew him well and often gave him soup or some food to eat. He was a frequent guest in their rooms, sitting for long hours near a warm stove. The day came when, with childish naiveté, he confessed to one of them that he was a Jew. Soon the secret spread throughout the Square, and it was not long before the Polish boys began to molest him. On one occasion they stole his cigarettes. The youngster ran to Bull, weeping bitterly.

"Show me which one did it."

"That one, in the jacket. . . ."

Bull approached the boy and demanded the cigarettes back.

"I didn't take them, I didn't hit him!" The Polish boy backed away and, throwing down the packet, took to his heels.

"If you pick on him again, we'll break your legs for you!" yelled Bolus's friends.

But the attacks began to occur more frequently. Finally, seeing that the defenders were always the same older boys, the Poles became suspicious and began to attack them as well. The situation grew worse daily and the danger increased. The Jewish boys grew cautious and kept away from each other and also from those Poles whom they suspected of evil intentions. Only Zbyszek disobeyed the rules, but his non-Jewish appearance and street-urchin's vocabulary saved him from serious trouble. In the meantime Bull advised Bolus to move to another part of town.

Bolus obeyed unwillingly and began to visit the Social Security building on Solec. There he spent each day sitting near some warm radiators in the waiting room. But after a few days of boredom he was back at the Square again, driven by his longing to be with the other boys and by a need to earn some money. He had become accustomed to his independence and to having money of his own. Seeing that Bolus could bring disaster on them all, the boys decided to collect 30 zlotys a day between them, and to pay Granny to keep him at home. At noon Bull would bring him some soup and in the evening when they all returned to sleep, he was given bread and butter. Bolus wept and begged to be allowed out, promising never to set foot on the Square and to stay near his radiators, but Bull remained adamant.

"Don't let him out, Granny, or I'll stop paying you," he ordered. So Bolus was stuck the whole day in the loft. Since he slept throughout the day, he plagued the others with questions when they returned at night. After a few days Granny, for reasons of her own, refused to keep him any longer. Bolus began roaming the streets once again and, craving friendly contact and a sympathetic ear, returned in spite of everything to Three Crosses Square. His arrival there coincided with my first visit to the children at the Square, described in an earlier chapter. Then, as was seen, Bolus was set upon by two Polish boys who accused him of being Jewish—and who aimed the same accusation at Bull when the latter intervened to rescue Bolus. So once again, for the group's safety, Bolus was banned from the Three Crosses Square.

Soon, another event made the problem of safety even more urgent.

"Zenek's been robbed of a packet of cigarettes," Pawel told Bull.

"Who did it?"

"The blond boy at the Square. He said if I yelled he'd tell everyone I was a Jew," explained Zenek.

"Does he know you? How did he find out?"

"I don't know."

"You must go away immediately. Find yourself another place, at least for a few days."

Zenek and his brother Pawel moved to Marszalkowska Street and took up a post at the corner of Hoza Street. At first they sold cigarettes, but changed soon after to newspapers. At noon they would hurry to the offices of the *Nowy Kurier Warszawski* (New Warsaw Courier) in Marszalkowska Street, where a large crowd of Polish boys waited for the papers. Everyone wanted to be first. With a bundle of newspapers under one arm they each jumped into passing trams and returned as fast as they could to Hoza Street.

Passersby, anxious for news from the front, quickly bought up the papers. Pawel and Zenek whetted their customers' curiosity by calling out sensational and often fictitious head-

117

lines: "German breaking away from the front! Front line shortened!"

A few days later there was indeed a tremendous sensation: the Resistance released a huge edition of a newspaper that was identical in appearance with the *Courier*. Under headlines announcing Spain's entry into the war were printed anti-German articles. Before the Germans or even the newsboys realised what had happened the whole edition was sold out. In front of the central station, under the very noses of unsuspecting gendarmes, the newsboys were selling these papers and getting twice or even four times the ordinary price per copy. In the evening the price went up to 50–100 zlotys a copy!

Pawel and Zenek made more money that day than in a whole month normally. The following day they had dinner in a first-class restaurant and in the afternoon bought underwear at the market. With the rest of the money they bought a stock of cigarettes. It was not in their nature to store money for a later day. In the evening they met the others at Granny's on Krucza Street, asked for news from the Square, and described their latest success.

By now I was an almost daily visitor at the Square. Gradually, I became acquainted with all the children, listening to their bargaining, admiring their skill and courage. My continuing visits to the Square met with a fairly favourable reception, and I began to obtain precise information about everything that took place at the Square, mainly through continuous contact with Bull.

The case of the cigarette sellers of Three Crosses Square remained on the agenda of the Jewish National Committee. We examined what forms our contact with them should take and what help we could offer. The attacks on Bolus and Zenek demonstrated the unceasing danger which threatened them all; and their situation was deteriorating daily. Bolus was now threatened openly and could bring disaster any minute.

The separation of Bolus from the others became an urgent task for the Organisation. Desperate efforts were made to find him a home, but unfortunately the question of a den was one of the most difficult problems of those times. It was not easy to find a Pole who would take in a Jew, even for a high fee. This was due to the Draconian methods introduced by the Germans, and to the great number of agents and Volksdeutsch zealots operating among the population. In the meantime I wanted to provide the boys with some funds, which they steadfastly refused. "What do we need money for? We may be gone tomorrow," said Bull.

The question of removing Bolus from the Square was our sole topic of conversation, the touchstone of our relationship. My full acceptance by the group and the allaying of their remaining suspicions as to my motives depended on the solution of this problem. Finally I discovered a widow, living in extreme poverty with her five small children, who agreed to take Bolus for a suitable fee. The sanitary conditions of her little room left much to be desired—but, pressed by necessity, I had no choice but to accept.

The same day I went to the Square accompanied by one of my charges dressed in the uniform of a night watchman. He was to help me lead the child from the Square to the Old Town.

Bull, Conky and Hoppy brought Bolus. He was trembling with cold and fright. The whole group of us hid in the entrance of a nearby house. The business of parting began. Bolus' friends arrived in a steady stream to give him a parting blessing. The little one cried. It was difficult for him to endure this sudden abandonment of the Square, particularly the parting from his friends. Most of the time he stood as if turned to stone, unable to react to their words. Bull tried to cheer him up. "Don't be frightened, you'll be better off than us."

"We'll meet after the war," was Teresa's message.

Finally I said "That's enough."

At that moment the last one, Toothy, arrived and pushed two white bread rolls and some sweets into Bolus' hands. I took Bolus by the sleeve but he refused to move. He wept, lifting imploring eyes to Bull and myself. All his friends wanted to visit him at least once a week but unfortunately I was not able to allow it. None of the group was to know his address— this was a basic principle of successful conspiracy. Knowledge of the address could mean great danger for Bolus and for his new guardians. The boys admitted the soundness of my arguments with a heavy heart; but they remained anxious, and made a plan which would ensure that they received regular news about him. Unknown to me, Bull handed Bolus five small slips of paper with his signature, asking the child to send one of them each week through me as a proof that he was alive and well.

After talking to Bull, Bolus followed me obediently. I led the way out of the house with Bolus following a few paces behind. As we left the Square, the boys' eyes followed our retreating figures.

At length we reached the house chosen for him. The walls of the little room were covered with cobwebs. The small children who were playing on the floor surrounded us. Their mother told them that a little cousin had arrived from the country. He had been orphaned recently and was to stay with them. Bolus listened calmly, understanding the implications of what she said and appreciating the situation. He was given a slice of black bread and put to play with the other children.

I quickly settled the formalities with the woman and was about to leave when Bolus caught my coat and would not let go. I promised to visit next day. When I left, Bolus sat sadly on the floor, refusing to play with the others, even refusing the bread.

By the next day, however he had brightened up a little. The surrounding misery helped him to get used to the new place. Soon he knew the names of all the children and took part in their games. When I came next afternoon, Bolus threw himself into my arms and burst into tears. Surprised by this greeting I held him, trying to calm him.

"Are you unhappy here? Why are you crying?"

A slight smile appeared on his face and I understood that these were tears of joy.

"It's good here! It's warm!" he said. "How is everybody at the Square?"

I felt that he longed for his friends, for freedom, even for the radiators in the Social Security building. He greeted me as a relative or as one of the cigarette boys. I stayed a long time telling him about the Square and how it would be after the war. Before leaving, I gave him a primer and encouraged him to learn to read.

A few days later I visited him again. This time I found him quite at home. He was playing with the other children and took no notice of my arrival.

"Well, Bolus, don't you want to go back to Three Crosses Square?" I asked.

He got up from the floor and smiled: "I'll go there when the Germans are gone," he said after some thought.

"And did you learn a lot from your primer?"

He nodded proudly.

"Would you like to write a letter to the boys, then," I proposed with a smile. He appeared confused and pulled out the five small slips of paper from his pocket.

"For Bull," he said. After a short talk with the woman I said goodbye to Bolus, promising to bring some more news from the Square.

I went straight to see the boys, thinking that the slips would be like a live greeting, replacing the letter he was still unable to write. I imagined their joy. I was therefore surprised by their reaction. They were clearly frightened. There was almost a panic. They talked among themselves, looking at me threateningly. I could not understand what had happened and could only guess hopelessly. I even thought they were about to attack me.

"Bolus must be gone," I heard Conky's voice suddenly.

"What's the matter? What are you afraid of?" I tried in vain to guess the reason for their anxiety. Even Bull looked severe and refused to talk to me.

121

"It's clear that something has happened to Bolus," he muttered finally.

"Not at all, Bolus is quite happy, he is doing fine." But my words failed to convince him.

"We want to see him, to make sure he is alive," said one of the boys.

"What are you talking about? It's dangerous. You must believe me that Bolus is all right." But I was unable to convince them.

"We don't want to talk to you," said the usually silent Frenchy.

Someone shouted in my direction: "We'll meet again!" Another added: "You'll pay for Bolus!"

That sounded dangerous. I tried to talk to them, to explain the stupidity of their suspicions, but it was in vain. The atmosphere was deteriorating minute by minute. I could see that an unfortunate move now could bring catastrophe. I began to retreat. I was thinking literally of flight and don't know how the whole thing would have ended if I had not jumped into a passing tram. From afar I saw the small group with their fists raised.

"Cat! We'll blow you!" I heard Zbyszek's voice.

I returned home that evening very depressed. The boys' confidence, gained with so much difficulty, was completely gone. I could not understand what had happened and what was the cause of our misunderstanding. That night I couldn't sleep. Various thoughts spun through my head; small slips of paper whirled before my eyes. "You've killed Bolus" rang in my ears. I knew the boys well enough to realise that without proof of Bolus' existence all further work with them was impossible. Furthermore, I was afraid that their vengeance might bring disaster on myself and even on the Organisation.

Realising that no argument would convince the boys now, I decided to show them that Bolus was all right. For a long time I deliberated on the best way out of the situation. To take one of the boys with me to the Old Town seemed too dangerous. In view of the catastrophic shortage of that kind of accommodation we could not afford to lose the den. In any case the assurance of one of the boys might not convince the others. There was only one way left: to bring Bolus back to the Square.

Early next morning I went to look for Bull and soon found him. But conversation was difficult.

"I shall bring Bolus today for a short visit so that everyone can see he is all right," I announced.

I arrived with the child (whom I had told not to reveal his hiding-place) at the appointed hour and the boys, overjoyed, surrounded us immediately, showering him with questions. They wanted to know everything: how was he living, what was he doing, was he well? "And where do you live?" asked someone.

"That man said if I tell you, he won't take me back."

"Why on earth did you give him all the slips of paper at once? You were supposed to send one a week," said Bull irritably.

Bolus could not explain and here the whole story came out. Excited by his new surroundings, Bolus had forgotten about their agreement, thus causing the whole unnecessary muddle. Seeing how completely unfounded were their suspicions, the boys tried eagerly to explain their behaviour and begged my forgiveness. From that moment on—they promised—nothing could shake their trust in me.

Bolus returned to the Old Town. Unfortunately, only a few days later it became necessary to find him a new home. The landlady's children fell ill and Bolus had to be removed so as to avoid infection. I told the boys about this new development and found unexpected help from Bull. His old friend, the teacher Idzikowski, had agreed suddenly to take Bolus. The fee presented no difficulty (Z.K.N. was generous with money for children) but Mr. Idzikowski's other conditions caused more trouble. Afraid of vermin, he insisted that the boy should arrive thoroughly cleaned up, and suitably dressed. He was not ready for the 'purification' to take place in his house. This complicated the whole matter. Finally, I agreed to take Bolus

123

to the public baths. Bull did the bathing and scrubbing and dressed the child in new clothes bought on the previous day.

We went to Grochow where Bolus, clean and in new clothes and with a beret on his head, made a good impression on his new guardian. He introduced himself as Boleslaw Wroblewski (the name on his false birth certificate) and quickly made friends with eight-year-old Januszek, Mr. Idzikowski's son. In the evenings his new guardian began to teach him to read and write. Bolus proved to be a bright pupil and after two months knew almost as much as Januszek, who was in the second grade.

From time to time I visited him, bringing toys and books and I gave detailed reports of his progress to the other boys.

Bolus' absence from the Three Crosses Square reduced the tension. Slowly everything returned to normal. The boys regained their courage and again fought ferociously with the Poles for every likely customer.

A few days after Bolus was moved to his new home, Bull informed me of the existence of the Amchu-man. Soon he was provided by me with false papers and money, which enabled him to move from his hole to a cellar belonging to a Polish friend. There he constructed a primitive but clever hide-out by knocking some planks together in the shape of a coffin and placing the construction in a corner. He covered it with straw on top and with old rags and scrap metal at the sides, and attached two rabbit cages to the front door. So he spent his days in the locked cellar, hiding in his box at the slightest noise. Every evening his host's wife brought him food, and I visited him now and again.

Zenek (left) and Pawel during the 1944 Uprising

Zenek, Israel, 1964

Pawel, Israel, 1961

Bolus, as Mrs. Kalot found him in 1942

Bolus, an officer in the Israeli army, 1962

Toothy (left) and Conky, Warsaw, 1944

Toothy, Canada, 1947

Conky, Israel, 1950

Easing of Tension

IN THE MEANTIME the Z.K.N. decided to provide the children with false birth certificates. But filling in the documents correctly posed a particular kind of problem. It may seem odd, but there existed a certain connection between an individual's physical appearance and the sound of his name. In general, though, the certificates were supposed to come from districts settled by Poles in areas beyond the river Bug, which made it impossible to verify their authenticity. Armed with this kind of paper, one could invent a story about one's family being sent to Siberia by the Bolsheviks. It was useful also to choose a name indicating peasant origins, which in turn could lead to a story about a cruel father or a village burnt down in the course of the fighting. Every child had to invent his own story and to be able to recite it without mistakes in every possible situation. Dates of birth were chosen so as to make them appear younger. Some of the children had been using false names for quite a time already and we completed their certificates accordingly.

Bull supplied me with false names, ages and characteristics for all the Jewish children in the Square. Then the blank certificates received from the Organisation had to be suitably completed. We employed several people to do this work, in order to avoid too much similarity of handwriting.

The receipt of these certificates was a great and joyous

125

occasion for the children. For most of them they were the first documents confirming their 'Aryanism'. However, we did not stop there; a few days later it was decided to provide school identity cards as well. This plan met with an obstacle: the children, fearing some kind of a trap, refused at first to let us have their photographs. Although they now trusted me personally, they had doubts as to the motives of the 'Polish woman from the Resistance', who was supposed to provide the documents. The explanations and arguments went on for days and it was Bull's vote which finally dispersed the last doubts.

The identity cards were authentic and appeared in the appropriate school registers. This was arranged by a Polish woman named Janina Buchholc. (Mrs. Buchholc looked after several Jews in hiding. In her Translations and Official Applications office on Miodowa Street she had organised a liaison point for the Jewish Resistance.) The children, now provided with birth certificates and school identity cards, grew more confident and began to move about freely, for they had papers to show in case of necessity. This was a decisive point in their lives.

The relationship with the Polish boys, whose doubts vanished at the sight of identity cards, improved steadily. Our boys added their own imaginary stories about school life, nasty teachers, playing truant and unfinished homework. They bragged about their skill in avoiding school and the more cheeky and outrageous their behaviour, the more respect they gained from the Poles.

At that time, Teresa ceased to be the only girl in the group. Mosze-Stasiek met Jasia, whom he had known in the ghetto, and brought her to the Square. At first she sold cigarettes like everyone else, but quite soon moved into a far more profitable line, dealing in vodka, either home-made or bought illegally from the Germans. These transactions took place in front of the grocery Julius Meinl—*Nur für Deutsche,* at the corner of the Three Crosses Square and Ksiazeca Street.

Jasia made enough money to be decently dressed, but her lack of papers hampered her movements in town and made it difficult to find shelter at night. However, as soon as she was provided with a false indentity card, she found a room with a family and had something to protect her in case of a street identity check. She was helped in her work by an attractive 15-year-old girl Halinka whom Jasia recognised in the street. Halinka was not too keen on the cigarette business.

"You've got to run about too much," she said. She wandered round the Square with nothing to do and her pretty face and trim figure attracted many admirers. Mosze-Stasiek, too, made approaches to the girl, while at the same time defending her from others. It was Bull who decisively stopped his amorous ambitions.

At that time the activities of the Polish Resistance reached new heights in Warsaw. Painted or chalked slogans appeared on walls and pavements: 'Poland shall win', the anchor (emblem of the Underground Movement), and the single words: *Verloren* and *Kaput*. On Three Crosses Square, the cigarette sellers, Polish and Jewish alike, were swept by patriotic fervour, chalking the anchor on the road and writing 'only pigs sit in the flicks' on the walls of the Apollo Cinema.

There were several armed attacks on the Germans and collaborators in various parts of the town. The Germans retaliated with severe measures against the civilian population. Hordes of SS and Gestapo combed the town, dragging people out of trams and searching flats, cellars and attics. The Three Crosses Square was not spared and the boys often had to hide in the garden of the Deaf and Dumb Institute or in the Church of St. Alexander.

During one such raid the Germans caught Mosze-Stasiek and drove him with hundreds of others to the provisional camp on Litewska Street. Panic descended on the boys as they feared that he might be forced to reveal their existence. They deserted the Square and scattered in small groups throughout the town. That night no one returned to sleep at Granny's or Mrs. Lodzia's or in any of the places known to Mosze-Stasiek; instead they slept in ruins, attics and cellars.

127

At this time Teresa once again tried to find shelter with Mrs. Kalot on Widok Street. The Polish woman must have taken a liking to the girl, since after such a long time she agreed to take her in permanently and even found her a job in a German mess kitchen on Jerozolimskie Avenue. Working in a German canteen, she was now above any suspicion. She cleaned, scrubbed floors and brought cigarettes and newspapers for the soldiers. There were other Polish girls working in the mess and Teresa made friends with one of them. They used to go home together, listening on the way to the street 'barker' (loudspeaker) and enjoying the news of German defeats at the front. On Sundays they went together to church. Teresa played the role faultlessly, but did not forget her friends; she visited them from time to time, showing great interest in their lives.

The brothers Pawel and Zenek found a Polish woman who, ignorant of their true identity, took them in and registered both according to their false papers. She saw to it that they said their prayers each night, and they went down on their knees obediently, muttering something indistinguishable. In the morning the two 'cousins', as they had introduced themselves to her, went to Marszalkowska Street where they sold cigarettes and newspapers.

One evening the landlady threw a party to which many guests were invited. One of them happened to come from Lwow.

"My boys are from Lwow too, you've got compatriots!" cried the landlady, remembering their birth certificates.

The guest drew the boys into a conversation, asking questions about their homes. Their confused answers awoke his suspicions. The following day the landlady interrogated both boys and they had to flee. Their papers were useless after that, and I provided them with new ones under different names.

Bull, Zbyszek, the Peasant and Frenchy moved their business to the Central Station. But the Polish cigarette sellers, whose leader was a fair-haired boy nicknamed 'Whitey,' did not welcome new competitors. Zbyszek, armed with a rich vocabulary of swear words, quickly reached an understanding with the leader but the others, uneasy, tried to avoid him as best they could. Unfortunately he was forever seeking them out on various pretexts and the Jewish boys, alarmed, suspected a trap. (When the war ended it transpired—to the astonishment of most of them—that Whitey too was a Jew.)

Hoppy, Conky, Toothy and little Stasiek found a spot in front of the Eastern Station, where together with Jurek and Wladek they sold cigarettes or exchanged postcards for cigarettes and tinned food with the German soldiers returning from the front. There, they met a red-haired nine-year-old boy also selling cigarettes. They sensed immediately that he was a Jew and tried to engage him in conversation.

"Do you know who I am? Can't you guess? challenged Toothy.

"Look at him, Carrot-top, just take a look and you'll know," added Jurek, pointing to Conky.

The child paled with fright and stepped back, fearing a trap.

"Don't be scared, we are 'amchu' too," whispered Conky.

After further reassurance, 'Carrot-top' admitted the truth and they chattered frankly about their lives. The boy confessed that the sale of cigarettes helped to keep his mother in her den on Brzeska Street. Lack of papers prevented her from leaving the house and the boy was in constant danger of chance arrest. Bull took his story to heart and informed me immediately about this new discovery.

A few days later Carrot-top and his mother were provided with false papers and money, and the grateful woman offered to do the laundry for all the cigarette boys from then on. This in turn helped the children's appearance enormously as well as improving their hygiene, and so lessened the suspicions aroused by their obvious neglect.

One day the news came that Mosze-Stasiek had escaped from the camp on Litewska Street and was back on the Three Crosses Square. This caused a sensation, and everybody ran to see him. He was thinner and his head was shaved, which gave the boys the idea of nicknaming him 'Baldy'. The Three

Crosses Square came to life again. The boys sold their cigarettes, as always quarrelling fiercely over each client. They returned to their old dens.

"I thought you'd all drowned," was Granny's curt greeting when they appeared on Krucza Street; but they knew that she was glad to see them alive.

The Polish boys at the Square asked the group about the reason for their absence, and each one invented his story. One was ill, another one's aunt had died; another had found a different place—a meeting point for Germans—and yet another had been arrested for selling adulterated cigarettes.

Only Mosze-Stasiek refused to go back to selling cigarettes. The fact that he had been taken for an adult by the Germans, and his escape from the camp, made him feel superior to the other boys. He took to visiting the tram conductors in their shelter, and they in turn offered him vodka and taught him card games. At times he appeared on the Square drunk, spreading panic among the boys. Nevertheless, he defended the younger Jewish boys from attacks, though he made them pay for it.

"Didn't you see me fighting for you?" he would boast.

The boys complained to Bull, who tried in vain to intervene.

"You don't expect me to risk my neck for nothing, do you?" was Baldy's reply. Encouraged by him, both the Jewish and Polish cigarette boys often spent all their money on drink in the nearby restaurant.

I was informed of these developments during my daily meetings with Bull. The case of Baldy was discussed at the meetings of the Z.K.N. It was impossible to isolate him from the others without his consent. In any case, he often came to the aid of the boys, so that moral considerations had to take second place. We therefore decided not to do anything about him.

In the meantime another winter was approaching and the boys were again suffering from the cold. They stamped their feet and, setting their trays on the pavement, beat their arms vigorously against their bodies. Each morning at the Rozycki bazaar where they ate their breakfast they looked around for warm second-hand clothes. The clothes they had brought with them from the ghetto no longer fitted them, since their food had begun to improve both in quantity and quality—so that everything they wore was skimpy and short as well as nearly worn out. Their earnings were fair, and together with the small sums received from me every month, sufficient for such purchases. Soon they bought new outfits—there was no shortage of used clothing at the market—and their appearance improved considerably. They also visited the baths at the Gigant more often than in the past.

It was during one of these visits that they ran into three boys at the entrance. Two of them looked suspicious.

Three from Praga

ONE OF THE BOYS at the Gigant was Izaak, who acquired the familiar nickname of Stasiek on the Aryan side. He began his career under that name as a shoe-shine boy at Central Station. There were several boys there, all working frantically to cope with the demand. One of them stood out from the others: quiet, silent and withdrawn, though he could when necessity arose swear as well as the rest of them. It was clear, however, that something was worrying him. His name was Romek, and he lived on Targowek; but in fact, since the death of his mother and his father's second marriage, he rarely slept at home. His father, an alcoholic, beat him up at the slightest provocation, his step-mother was malicious and cruel and in the end Romek ran away from home and began wandering the streets.

Izaak-Stasiek befriended him and told him a story about his own father—that he had been deported for forced labour to Germany—and about his mother who was living with a gentleman friend. The two boys found they had a lot in common and became inseparable. In the daytime they cleaned shoes for the German soldiers, and at night they went together to sleep in the ruins. Izaak-Stasiek bore the discomforts of their existence in silence, but Romek, though quiet during the day, would not stop complaining at night. Yet he had voluntarily exchanged a comfortable bed for damp cellars and cold ruins. In contrast to Izaak-Stasiek he had a home to return to, but his pride prevented him from doing so.

The boys found a good shelter in a large metal rubbish container, but after two weeks were chased away by one of the municipal refuse collectors. Soon afterwards they moved to Sucha Street where there were army barracks and assembly points. After the day's work they crept in to the allotments of the Staszic colony and slept in the huts there.

Two months later they were discovered by a night watchman and again had to look for a new shelter. The large crate of sand at the corner of Sucha and Filtrowa Streets seemed just right. They threw out the contents and installed themselves inside, covered with their jackets. But it was bitterly cold inside and the rain seeped in. Wet through, they ran in the morning to the barracks to warm themselves over the little charcoal stove.

Then one day Izaak-Stasiek met a friend from the ghetto, 14-year-old Kuba. Kuba told him his story—how after the first action he had escaped from the ghetto with his two sisters (Stefcia and Marysia, whom we already know from Three Crosses Square). They sang in streets and restaurants, and did quite well. He himself joined up with a group of street-singers with whom he now wandered around Warsaw and was also doing quite well.

"How did you get here?" asked Izaak-Stasiek. "And what about a den?"

"I sleep in Gigant on Jagiellonska Street."

"They let you in?"

"I tipped the caretaker 10 zlotys and told him I was evacuated from the Reich. He fixed my registration. If you haven't got a den you can come with me, we'll manage somehow."

Izaak-Stasiek liked the idea but had scruples about Romek.

"Should I leave him?" he wondered. "But if I take him with us he may find out I am a Jew. . . . He can always return home, to his family, while I. . . ."

He decided to accept Kuba's invitation. That day he worked more cheerfully, whistling from time to time. Even Romek was surprised.

"Why are you so happy?"

"Tonight I'm going to sleep in a real bed," boasted Izaak-Stasiek. He gave Romek a story that his family had requested him to sleep at home.

In the evening Izaak-Stasiek went with Kuba to Gigant. The caretaker, receiving his 10 zlotys, took the boy to the office where one of the Albertine brothers in charge of the place registered all newcomers.

"I have been evacuated from Bydgoszcz," began Izaak-Stasiek. "I ran away from home because my step-mother beat me. My name is Stanislaw Kowalczyk but my papers have been stolen. . . ."

"Yes, that is so, I know him," confirmed the caretaker. And so Izaak-Stasiek was registered.

The two boys entered an enormous ward. In the poor light of the single electric bulb, it looked like a huge prison cell. Rows of double bunks lined the walls. Unshaven and dirty faces peered round with infected eyes. Several hundred men came here for the night, the majority of whom belonged to the criminal underworld, though some were very old men or cripples. Bottles of home-made vodka or methylated spirits stuck out of their pockets. Fights were a daily—or rather nightly—occurrence. A newcomer, ignorant of the local customs, found himself in the morning without clothes or shoes, which he had to buy back with vodka. Every morning the monks distributed bread and hot tea, and on Sundays they herded the whole crowd to church. Kuba, who had a pleasant voice, was taken in to the choir. So from wandering round the streets on weekdays singing begging-songs, he turned on Sundays to the singing of hymns!

In time, however, suspicion about Kuba's origins began to grow. At first expressed in cutting remarks and petty maliciousness, it soon assumed serious proportions; and the boy, aware of the threatening danger, decided to leave Warsaw. He met a peasant at the market who agreed to take him on as a farm hand, where he remained until the Liberation.

Izaak-Stasiek found it difficult to get used to the atmosphere in Gigant, but he was pleased to have a roof over his head, and this influenced his general outlook and his enthusiasm for work. He often sang while cleaning shoes and he told Romek various tales; that he had a comfortable bed, that his mother spoiled him and her lover offered him sweets.

Days passed one after another. Stasiek's only worry was caused by frequent police visits, checking documents in Gigant. Several times the police laid siege to the 'holy place' and forced everyone to flee to the bathhouse. For this reason he regularly arrived late at night, and if the sudden checks found him already there, he escaped—with the caretaker's help—through a side door. But the caretaker realised that the boy had something on his conscience and made him pay with vodka. Izaak-Stasiek, unable to find another shelter, was forced to comply—though he pretended to do so of his own free will so as not to increase the man's suspicions.

One evening as he returned to the shelter he met another friend from the ghetto, 14-year-old Leon. He was blue with cold, so Izaak-Stasiek brought him to Gigant where the usual procedure of bribing the caretaker to obtain registration took place. The newcomer, happy to have a roof over his head, lay down to sleep. His awakening in the morning was equally happy when the monks gave him a breakfast he had not had for a long time.

A few days later, while Izaak-Stasiek was lying on his bunk and sewing his torn jacket, another boy walked into the ward. It was difficult to recognise his face in the poor light, and only when the newcomer approached him did Stasiek recognise Romek. He held his breath and tried to cover his face with his jacket but it was too late. Their eyes met and Romek approached the bunk.

"What are you doing here?" he asked. "You said you were sleeping at home."

Izaak-Stasiek was silent. Romek looked him in the face and

then turned his eyes to Leon who was lying beside him. Suspicion dawned in his mind.

"Lie down here, I'll explain everything," said Izaak-Stasiek finally. "But swear you won't tell anyone," he added.

After a long preamble Izaak-Stasiek confessed that he was a Jew. It did not make a great impression on Romek, who was hurt only because, as he said, "We are friends and you didn't trust me."

Izaak-Stasiek tried to justify himself. Finally, they made peace and from that day on their friendship grew even stronger.

The following day Izaak-Stasiek and Romek went to town to work as usual while Leon went begging in the shops. He entered Mrs. Jappo's restaurant on Szeroka Street.

"I'm an orphan. Please help," he whispered at the threshold. The owner gave him a hostile stare.

"So young and already begging. Get to work! Don't loiter in the streets!"

"I looked for work but couldn't find any."

"Come here tomorrow then, I'll find something for you to do," she offered, mollified.

The following day Leon sat at a low stool in the kitchen, wrapped in a large apron, and peeled potatoes. He worked for his keep and in the evening the owner gave him chops left over from the dinner. He took them to Gigant for his friends, who now called him 'Chopper'.

Izaak-Stasiek and Romek soon left their shoe-brushes to try their hand at business. Some German soldiers where stationed on Szeroka Street near Gigant, and the boys began by buying cigarettes, tinned food or underwear from them and then selling what they got at the Rozycki market. Later on they established contact with a member of the Polish Resistance and on his orders bought army uniforms and overcoats. A few days later the gendarmerie surprised them at the barracks and the boys barely escaped with their lives. They moved on to Tlomackie, outside what used to be the Jewish Library, but which now housed German army stores. There they bought large quantities of uniforms from one of the soldiers and transported them by drozki to Bednarska Street, to an address indicated by their Resistance contact. Each one of these transports was a dangerous exploit.

From their contact, the boys received a false Todt Organisation* certificate. But this was no trivial journey. Izaak-Stasiek and Romek, wearing Todt uniforms with swastikas on their sleeves, would sit on the sacks of goods, their faces radiating importance. The most difficult thing was when the contacts were changed, and then it was necessary to travel with the dangerous goods to Praga—to 36 Jagellonska Street or to 19 Minska Street, where the new contact would receive the goods.

One evening in December 1943, the boys were sitting with grave faces on the bags of contraband when a gendarme stopped their drozki on the Kerbedz bridge. Izaak-Stasiek jumped off the cab and approached the gendarme, greeting him with Heil Hitler. In broken German he reported that he was transporting uniforms and overcoats to his unit on Praga, and showed his Todt certificate. The gendarme asked to see the transport permits and Stasiek calmly explained that these documents were carried by the lieutenant who was travelling by tram. With cold cheek he invited the gendarme to get into the drozki and come with them to Praga to investigate on the spot. The gendarme, believing his story, allowed them to go. All this took only a few minutes. Yet a single wrong word or movement could have caused a tragedy. But the boys were not in the least put off by this incident. Their task accomplished and money in their pockets, they returned to Gigant where they were joined by Chopper.

The three boys went on to the baths, at which point they first met some of the cigarette sellers from the Three Crosses Square. They had their baths and then invited the Praga boys to the Three Crosses Square.

"What do you do?" asked Izaak-Stasiek.

"We sell cigarettes. Come with us, you'll see," boasted Bull.

---

* A German employment organisation, engaged in construction works for the army, employing some Poles, including those under age.

The baths over, they all went to the Square. It looked as though the band had increased. In a sudden access of good humour and healthy appetite, they decided to celebrate at a nearby restaurant. Zbyszek proposed a quarter of vodka. Romek, whom the cigarette boys immediately adopted as one of theirs, agreed with enthusiasm.

"I can see you are all bright boys, you're doing fine!" he exclaimed. "We too are doing business with the Germans. We sleep at the Gigant . . . . If you haven't got a den, come to the Gigant too. I'll fix it," proposed Izaak-Stasiek, whom the boys from the Square had nicknamed Stasiek-from-Praga to avoid confusion with the other Stasiek.

His offer came just in time, as an unfortunate incident had occurred at Granny's the previous night. After a full day of successful work, the boys arrived in good moods. Having settled the formalities, they climbed up to the loft and were fooling around on their beds in high spirits when suddenly the rotten planks gave way under their weight and the whole crowd fell to the floor, raising clouds of dust and bruising some of them.

Granny swore to high heaven. There was a terrible row.

The boys were afraid that the noise would bring the tenants in, but fortunately there were no further complications. They spent the night sitting on the floor in the corner of the room and in the morning set about rebuilding the loft. They worked hard the whole day (and had in fact gone to the baths to clean up after this) but they were still afraid of the old woman's reaction.

So Zbyszek and the Peasant, the main culprits, gladly accepted Stasiek-from-Praga's invitation and moved to Gigant the same day.

Conditions in the doss house were fairly comfortable. It was difficult to see clearly in the poor light and Romek took on the role of spokesman when it was necessary to talk to other inmates or to the authorities. He was an excellent representative and he was happy to belong to the 'family'. Thus the gang became an even stronger group with many sturdy lads.

This brought them all a sense of self-confidence and well-being. But in those days such feelings seldom lasted long in the face of the ever-present danger.

Towards the end of February 1944, the German gendarmes came to the Gigant to arrest Stasiek-from-Praga. Obviously someone had denounced him for his dealing in army uniforms. Fortunately he was not in at the time, but from that day on he could no longer return there. He moved on to a Polish woman at 18 Bugaj Street. He paid her 100 zlotys per month, but then committed an error by giving her his real name—Stanislaw Kowalczyk—which was on the German list of wanted persons. When his landlady demanded his registration, he tried to postpone it by every possible means, but she began to suspect that he had something on his conscience. She threatened to throw him out and Stasiek, having nowhere to go, paid her off in money and gifts.

After a few days I was able to supply him with new documents in the name of Stanislaw Wisniewski. He explained the change in his name by his membership of the Polish Resistance. The woman believed him, and her suspicions were lulled further when from time to time he brought home German uniforms which she dyed and sold at the market, getting an additional income.

One day Stasiek-from-Praga and Romek, walking down Jasna Street, ran into a 16-year-old boy in front of the Restaurant 'Morskie Oko', ('Eye of the Sea') where he worked as a page boy. They realised immediately that he was a Jew and talked him into joining the band. The boy, who introduced himself as Maisterek ('Fixer'), began helping Stasiek and Romek in transporting the German uniforms for the Polish Resistance, and money kept coming in. They would suddenly appear in the Square in the uniform of the Todt organisation, wearing swastikas, making a huge impression on the Polish boys, and adding to the feeling of security and pride of their Jewish comrades.

Those who Perished

JOSEF SZINDLER—HOPPY, BORN 1928
KAZIK GELBLUM—FRENCHY, BORN 1929
ROMUALD PLONKOWSKI—ROMEK, BORN 1929

At that time a few of the boys found an additional source of income by selling theatre tickets. They bought them an hour before the performance at the News theatre, at 73 Mokotowska Street, and sold them when all the others were gone, for a much higher price.

On one occasion two of them were left with unsold tickets, and they looked in vain for late customers.

"Come on, fellows, don't worry, we'll go instead, haven't we got a right?" said Mosze-Stasiek (Baldy).

Hoppy, Zbyszek and Toothy went in with him, but the way was barred by one of the ushers.

"Out of here, you bastards," he yelled.

"There are no bastards here," replied Zbyszek.

"At least I am my mother's bastard, while you . . . ." added Baldy.

"But we have tickets," explained Hoppy.

The matter was referred to the director, who decided to let the boys in. This was the first time they had been in a theatre. Proudly, they marched in and took their seats in the front

140

row. People stood up to look at them. Surely no one thought that they could be Jews. The boys stayed right till the end of the performance, passing ironic comments about the actors, to the great amusement or disapproval of the audience, many of whom knew them from the Three Crosses Square.

Back in the street they discussed the performance. "Those comedians were almost like circus clowns," said one of them.

In the evening at Granny's the boys, proud of their exploit, boasted to the others. But Bull told them off for unnecessarily attracting the attention of so many people. To their argument that they had 'regular' papers, he replied by pointing out Hoppy's Semitic features, adding that the papers were only a protection and should not tempt them to behave in such a fool-hardy way.

Soon he was proved right, for a few days later Hoppy noticed that he was being followed. Bull, whom he told about it, advised him to stay at the Square as much as possible. This didn't help. A few young shmalzers, aged between 14 and 15 years, caught him in Jerozolimskie Avenue and followed him to the Square. Laying in wait near the church, they noticed a few other boys with Semitic features, caught them and robbed them of their money and cigarettes. The elder boys, with 'good' features, came to their aid. Baldy even drew blood from one of the attackers. The shmalzers retreated from the Square, only to return a few hours later.

The battle started again. This time not only the Semitic-looking boys but also the 'Poles' who defended them were attacked. The battle went on for some time and ended with the defeat of the shmalzers. They retreated but promised to return again the following day. The boys called for reinforcements from Praga.

The following day the whole band appeared at the Square. Romek and Stasiek-from-Praga, wearing the overcoats of the Todt organisation, strolled around waiting for the arrival of the shmalzers. Soon they appeared and pounced on Hoppy demanding money. There were four of them. The elder boys ran to help and pushed the attackers into the entrance of a house. After a short exchange of arguments, Romek set about them with a stick while Baldy and Bull helped with their fists. The shmalzers took to their heels, but were stopped in the entrance by Stasiek-from-Praga, who sent them on their way with a few healthy kicks.

"If you pick on any of the boys again I'll kill you!" he yelled after the attackers.

The cigarette boys returned to the Square proud of their victory. But the shmalzers had not given in. The attacks on Jewish boys continued. A dangerous situation arose, just as at the time of the trouble with Bolus. Again we had to clear the air and lessen the tension by isolating some of the boys. We were able to overcome the difficulty within a few days by finding a suitable den, when I managed to persuade Mrs. Lodzia at Saska Kepa to take in three boys. Since Toothy had been sleeping at her house for some months past, we left him there as the first, adding those in the most immediate danger: Hoppy and 'little' Stasiek.

Hoppy found it hard to leave the Square, but the other boys persuaded him to do so for safety's sake. He found Teresa particularly hard to leave, especially as she had taken the place of his sister Basia, but she too joined in persuading him. In the event the boys were happy at Mrs. Lodzia's. They spent their days in her neat little room, hiding in the lavatory at the sound of footsteps. The woman taught them reading, writing and arithmetic from books which I supplied. All the costs of their upkeep and studies were met by the Jewish National Committee (Z.K.N.). Hidden in their den, they were not allowed to come to the Square for fear of revealing the hiding-place. But I visited them with Bull every week, to give them all the news of the others.

Before leaving the house, Mrs. Lodzia always left them something to do. She set out their homework, or left them dishes to wash. Little Stasiek gladly carried out her instructions, but Toothy and Hoppy caused the good woman a lot of trouble. Well fed and rested, they could not sit still. They felt almost safe in the out-of-the-way corner in which they now lived, and as soon as the door closed behind Mrs. Lodzia they would leave their books and appointed tasks and look for something more interesting.

On one ocasion after Mrs. Lodzia had left, Toothy and Hoppy began a game of checkers. They soon grew bored, however, and began searching for something else. In the corner of the room stood an old-fashioned chest of drawers with a large mirror. Next to it hung a painted metal dish with a landscape on it.

"Let's see who can throw best," proposed Toothy, throwing a slipper. The plate gave out a metallic sound.

"Your go," he turned to Hoppy.

Hoppy picked up a shoe brush and threw it. This time a different sound rang out in the room, and two lines marked the mirror across its length and breadth. The boys jumped up, touched the broken glass and, frightened, looked at each other.

"What's going to happen now? Let's run!" cried Hoppy.

They vanished, leaving little Stasiek weeping in a corner. They went straight to the Three Crosses Square, where Bull heard their story and ordered them to return immediately. Toothy took a tram and went back, but Hoppy was too scared. In his childish imagination the broken mirror grew to the dimensions of a serious crime. He wandered round the Square for nearly an hour before finally agreeing to return. But he was never to return to the Saska Kepa sanctuary. He disappeared on the way there, in unknown circumstances. No one knows what happened to him, though two days later a Polish boy selling cigarettes at the Square told us that he had seen Hoppy in Szuch Avenue, being led by a Ukrainian soldier towards the Gestapo.

As usual Zbyszek could not refrain from joking. "Death to all mugs! I bet there is a cross growing over him now. This is the Three Crosses Square—well, we've got one cross already!"

The boys looked at each other, embarrassed. Bull broke the silence with: "Be careful, or there will be a cross growing over you too."

At that time the Z.K.N. began collecting the memoirs of war experiences. Its members tried to encourage their charges to write. This gave those in hiding a useful occupation and at the same time enriched the archives of the organisation with new material. Some of the children were encouraged to write their diaries by the promise of various prizes. Since Toothy could write I got him to work and the interesting diary of his experiences in the ghetto uprising was sent to the Z.K.N. archives.

Winter had passed and spring too was drawing to a close. Because of the fast changes at the eastern front and the allied offensive in the West, interest in the war news was growing. Some of the cigarette sellers changed to trade in newspapers.

"Germans breaking away from the enemy! Evacuation planned!" They called out headlines to encourage customers. Passers-by bought up papers bearing news of German defeats. The front was moving west. In private conversation, German soldiers often complained about the war and declared themselves to be against their Führer.

The cigarette boys found it easy to buy military equipment from them. The soldiers wanted money for girls. They wanted some fun before leaving for the front. The sight of thousands of wounded soldiers transported from the eastern front inspired no optimism.

In the middle of the second half of May 1944, Frenchy was standing by the Y.M.C.A. building with his cigarettes when an SS man from Alsace, who had known him in Paris, noticed him. The SS man invited Frenchy to a restaurant. It was a long time since the boy had eaten such a meal. Then they went on to the Apollo cinema to see a film about love, which Frenchy enjoyed. When the film was over, the German invited the boy to his house, saying that he wanted to show him photos from the front. Frenchy, unsuspecting, agreed. He even boasted to some of his colleagues about this new friend. And before the boys had time to react, to find Frenchy and dissuade him from going, the German was already dragging Frenchy towards Szuch Avenue and the Gestapo. He was never seen again.

The cigarette boys were deeply shaken. They could not understand his carelessness. Again there was panic at the Square as the boys feared that Frenchy might give them away under torture. Only Zbyszek seemed unimpressed.

"Didn't I tell you? Now we've got a second cross. I wonder who'll be the third," he joked.

At this point Bull lost his patience, and slapped Zbyszek with all his force in the face.

The cigarette boys left the Square and the dens known to Frenchy. They deserted Granny and Mrs. Lodzia. They wandered round town alone or in pairs, sleeping in ruined houses and in attics. They lost touch with each other, except for occasional meetings in the streets or at the river, where under the hot sun they lay in the sand or played in the water. During one of their games little Stasiek found himself too far from the shore and began drowning. Hearing his cries, the others jumped in to help. Romek who was nearest, and a good swimmer, pulled him out half-conscious to the surface, but at the same moment was himself stricken with cramp. And before the others realised what was happening Romek was caught by the undertow and drowned.

The boys stood thunderstruck. Suddenly one of them began calling for help. The water-police arrived and the boys who looked particularly Semitic had to leave. They watched the search from the safety of the Poniatowski Bridge, while the others helped the police. Up to their chins in water, they searched the river bed with long sticks, but in vain. Darkness interrupted the search. There was no hope of saving the boy. Only then did they realise that they had lost their best friend, a faithful companion in misfortune and a defender in their difficulties.

The body floated to the surface the following day, near Pelcowizna. The funeral took place two days later. In the procession beside Romek's family marched Stasiek-from-Praga,

145

Bull, Baldy and Zbyszek. On the grave Stasiek lay a bouquet bought collectively by all the boys.

My contact with the cigarette sellers was greatly hampered after they left the Square. Previously I had been able to follow all their movements and was aware of every change in their lives. In case of danger I was able to act quickly to separate a threatened boy or to supply new documents. Now, trying to find individual children in various parts of the town put me in a very uncomfortable and dangerous position. In these conditions the guardianship of the Organisation could not develop successfully. An unpleasant incident with Baldy added to my troubles.

I met the boy accidentally at Nowy Swiat. He was very nervous and I felt that he must have had trouble somewhere. He abruptly demanded a new set of papers for a different name, his old ones having been blown in circumstances he was unable to explain. He was impatient and pressing. I did not attach any importance to this and, taking his photograph for the identity card, promised to deliver the papers the following day. (The production of false documents was going fairly smoothly.) Suddenly I was surprised by another demand.

"I must have 1,500 zlotys a month—otherwise I'll know what to do."

This sounded almost like blackmail. For several months now Baldy had been receiving 500 zlotys, and this should have been sufficient for a modest existence. I tried to explain that he was given as much as every other adult Jew, but he remained unmoved.

"I demand 1,500 zlotys," he insisted. I judged all further arguments to be unnecessary.

I promised to pass on his demand to the appropriate authority and we arranged our next meeting. The Organisation debated at length on the measures to be taken to curtail his dangerous inclinations. Finally, we agreed on a fairly drastic procedure.

Instead of myself, two men went to see Baldy at our appointed meeting place. They recognised him at once from the photograph I supplied and took him into a house entrance. He defended himself vigorously but was subdued by a smart slap on the face. One of the men, gun in hand, stood at some distance, while the other read the Organisation's death sentence—apparently passed on Baldy for blackmailing Jews.

The boy paled and begged to be let off. He kissed their hands, wept and fell to his knees. After a short debate the two men agreed to suspend the sentence since he had shown his repentance. Baldy never suspected that the whole thing was an act.

"If we hear that you've picked on someone else you'll be shot immediately," they threatened on parting. The threat proved effective.

The incident with Baldy made us consider new ways of caring for the boys which would be more suitable to their changed conditions. Soon we found an excellent solution. After a great deal of effort we managed to establish contact with Mrs. Dargielowa, director of the R.G.O. bureau at 10 Widok Street. She agreed to help with the children, since they already had Aryan documents, and registered them with the R.G.O. as Polish orphans. Many of the children forgot the names of their supposed parents while giving the necessary information and Mrs. Dargielowa prompted efficiently, whispering suitable substitutes. A few days later the children received coupons for midday meals at the 'Housewives' restaurant in Nowy Swiat. They assembled at noon every day from all corners of the town and exchanged news about their work and experiences.

We thought also about helping them with their clothes. Although the majority were equipped by their own efforts, clothes and especially shoes did not last long in their way of life. So, receiving the necessary sum from Z.K.N., I bought suits of underwear, shoes and as much clothing as I could. I prepared parcels in my 'office' on Sedziowska Street, labelling them with the Aryan name of each child. The parcels were then distributed among the cigarette sellers through Mrs.

Dargielowa, to whom they all came now every fortnight to collect their money.

Meanwhile the front line was moving West. The force of the Soviet attacks was growing. The eastern part of Poland was witnessing very heavy fighting. Every day brought more names of liberated towns. The sound of artillery fire became stronger and the earth reverberated. People left the endangered zones, carrying only the barest essentials with them.

Bull met some Polish boys who enrolled him in the Underground Youth Organisation, the 'Grey Ranks'. He attended their meetings at 50 Polna Street, where the leader, 'Miroslaw,' conducted military exercises and political talks. The boys undertook liaison duties and assisted in what was called a minor sabotage operation. They also distributed conspiratorial literature and posted anti-German proclamations on the walls. These activities exposed Bull to a twofold danger but they also gave him full satisfaction. The sight of Germans fleeing in panic announced the approaching freedom. Rumour of the uprising was spreading.

Some of the survivors in 1945: left to right, Fixer, Halinka, and Bull (back row); Stasiek-from-Praga, Toothy, and Chopper (front row)

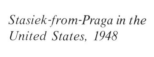

Stasiek-from-Praga in the United States, 1948

Zenek in the Israeli army, 1948

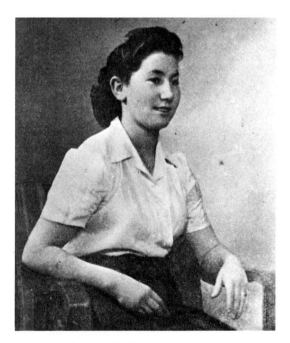

Teresa in Israel, 1947

The Threshold of Freedom

TENSION WAS MOUNTING from hour to hour. Foreseeing heavy fighting in Warsaw, I advised the boys to move out east of the Vistula. Some of them refused categorically.

"We want to join in the uprising!"

My reasoning had no effect. They considered themselves adult and were eager to fight the Germans. When I complained, the only exception they would make was Bolus. And shortly Mr. Idzikowski and his family, Bolus included, moved out to their summer villa in Michalin. By this time the Soviet and Polish armies were liberating the lands east of the Vistula. They had taken Lublin and now approached Warsaw.

The unit of Grey Ranks to which Bull belonged received orders to break through the front line. The boys were issued with arms and marched east in battle array. Bull was happy in the thought that at last he would be able to avenge the death of his family. He dreamed of an armed encounter with the enemy.

In the morning of 29th July, 1944, the unit pushed forward towards Pilawa, which was already in the hands of the Red Army. They had barely reached Garwolin before the first Soviet tanks got there. Thus it happened that the first of the cigarette sellers to be liberated was Bull, their leader.

149

He could not believe his eyes. He wanted to rejoice—but something weighed heavily on his mind. It was not thus that he had imagined the moment of liberation. The nightmare of the occupation was over, as was his fear and his need to maintain double identity. He was a whole human being at last, but he was the only one left of his entire family. He had never thought of this before, his fight for survival having left him no time to think. Now he looked on sombrely as others celebrated their freedom. He envied them. With tears running down his cheeks, he stood watching the passing tanks until clouds of dust hid them from view. The armed might rolled on towards Warsaw. At the same time Kuba was liberated in a village near Zambrow. Wladek and Jurek, who were hiding with a few more Jews in a bunker in Swidev, were liberated by the Red Army on 30th July.

Bolus was hiding in the cellar of the Idzikowski's family villa. He had had some difficult moments, as the suburb was in an area of fierce battles. The little houses were shaken by the explosion of shells and bombs. The hail of machine gun fire pruned the trees in the area. Finally, on the 2nd August, the first Soviet armour entered.

Carrot-top and his mother hid on Brzeska Street in Praga. Zbyszek was in Gigant. Conky found himself at Saska Kepa. He went to 3 Poselska Street to the house of one Chmielczyk, where he met up with little Stasiek, who had been moved there from Mrs. Lodzia's house, at 5 Radziwilowska Street. Toothy remained at Mrs. Lodzia's.

The front neared Praga. The inhabitants of the endangered areas were forced to flee for their lives, taking only their most important belongings with them. Toothy found a small hand-cart and began to make a living by carrying things. Conky and Little Stasiek were forced by Mr. Chmielczyk under threat of expulsion to accompany him on his raids on abandoned houses.

On 14th September Praga and Saska Kepa were liberated. Among the first units to enter Saska Kepa were some Jewish soldiers. Toothy, Conky and little Stasiek were free. Their joy knew no bounds. They threw themselves into the arms of the first Jew they met, a soldier in the Polish Army. They were no longer afraid that someone might denounce them. They enjoyed the air and the sunshine, even the rags they wore. They went into the street and began to look for the rest of their friends. They met Bull, who had now returned from Garwolin, in Grochow.

The very same day they met Carrot-top on Brzeska Street. Again they embraced. They paid no attention to the continuing artillery fire from the Germans on the left bank of the Vistula. Other people hid in cellars, but the boys disregarded danger as if it did not concern them. They spent the night in a tram shelter, still having nowhere to sleep. In the morning they were again on the streets, unwashed, tired after a sleepless night, but full of life and energy.

News of the Jewish children who had been saved spread like wildfire. People came to look at them as if they were museum exhibits. They were offered food and sweets. The Soviet and Polish soldiers and officers looked at them with wonder and asked about their experiences in the greatest detail but the boys had no time for confidences. Something else was on their minds. They wanted to see Bolus as soon as possible. One of the officers yielded to their pleas and drove them in his jeep to Michalin.

Their meeting with Bolus was touching in the extreme. The boys wept with joy, kissed and hugged the child, who seemed to resist their excessive outbursts. But the boys caught him and before Mr. Idzikowski had time to intervene they threw him up to the ceiling. Hurrah! Hurrah!

Slightly stunned, Bolus could not understand what was happening to him. Bull poked him in the ribs. "Well now, shall we go to the Three Crosses Square?" The whole company burst out laughing.

A few days later, being informed that a Jewish Committee had been set up in Lublin, they travelled there immediately. The Committee's house there, at 19 Lubartowska Street, was alive with survivors and returnees from Russia who had come with the Polish army. Everyone was looking for relatives among the names on the walls—filled with notices of families sought. For many hours the boys scanned the lists of the survivors, but did not find any of their own families. Suddenly Toothy cried out "Look, there's Amchu!" After the embraces and cries of wonder, they spent some time relating to each other their experiences during the last days of the occupation. In the evening the boys met Wladek and Jurek. They all went to the nearby restaurant where a feast had been arranged for them. A few days later Conky was informed that his two sisters had been saved in one of the villages in the suburbs of Warsaw.

On the 29th September a group of Warsaw rebels arrived in Lublin after crossing the Vistula (their positions in Powisle had been occupied). Among them was Mosze Stasiek—Baldy—who had immediately volunteered for the rebel army in the first days of the revolt.

In fact, the population of Warsaw had risen to arms on the 1st of August. The fight of the insurgents against the overwhelming forces of the enemy, armed to the teeth, was savage and bloody. Those of the cigarette boys who were caught by the events on the left bank, reported immediately to the recruiting stations. They wanted to do their duty.

Teresa, her Polish girl friend and Halinka joined the Red Cross. The sisters Marysia and Stefcia were accepted as runners with the Girl Guides. They carried letters and reports from one sector to another, often under German machine gun fire. Stefcia found somewhere a small revolver which she proudly showed to the soldiers. Under the nickname of 'Kaytek' she was the apple of their eye. The Peasant was surprised by the uprising on Hoza Street near the Three Crosses Square, and joined the platoon of Lieutenant 'Topor', at first as a runner, though he was later allowed to take part in the sorties to the Frascati Garden. Later on he was incorporated in the fighting unit as a regular soldier under the nickname of 'Pistol'.

Chopper fought on Mokotowska Street in the detachment of Major Sarna. But the greatest activity was shown by the brothers Pawel and Zenek. At the start of the uprising they were both on Bracka Street near Jerozolimskie Avenue. They reported immediately to a recruiting station but were turned away because of their age. They refused to give up, though, and hung around the whole day near the barricade, making themselves useful to the soldiers and awaiting the moment when they too would be needed. The occasion presented itself quite soon.

The Germans made up fortified positions in several buildings, among them the National Economy Bank (B.G.K.) on the corner of Jerozolimskie Avenue (which from the first day of the revolt had its name changed to General Sikorski Avenue) and Nowy Swiat. From there they fired on the insurgents' positions with light and heavy weapons. Jerozolimskie Avenue was swept by fire on two sides from the bank building, and from the Central Station became No Man's Land. In the middle of the road lay two dead Germans and near them two rifles and several grenades. These arms, so necessary for the insurgents, had to be brought in despite the range of fire. Pawel volunteered. The lieutenant commanding the section agreed, after some hesitation, to send him out on this dangerous assignment.

After midnight Pawel crawled out from the ruined house on the corner of Bracka Street into the centre of the road. The Germans, probably hearing a suspicious noise, fired a rocket. Pawel lay still, pretending to be dead. A few shots were fired, followed by silence and darkness. The boy shook off his fear and crawled nearer the dead men. He attached the rifles and grenades to his belt, took the bullets out of their pouches and stored them in his pocket, and crawled away from the dangerous zone. For this exploit, both brothers were accepted into the ranks of the insurgents. They were registered under their family name of Borkowski. Pawel was nicknamed 'Urchin', and Zenek 'Mickey'.

They were attached to the section's H.Q. as runners. The boys, proud of this honour, fulfilled their duties with the utmost enthusiasm. Thanks to their experiences and the

153

shrewdness they had acquired during their days of smuggling
—and, of course, during their eventful existence on the Aryan
side—they were second to none in bravura. They were often
to be found in the first line of fighting, and were especially
singled out for praise for their heroism by the command.

Several dead and wounded lay on the road in Jerozolimskie
Avenue. No one dared approach them or bring help. To show
oneself above the barricade could mean death. On the 10th
August, the insurgents captured a German Army pastor who
agreed to write a letter to the command in B.G.K., asking for
ceasefire while the dead and wounded were removed. Zenek
(Little Mickey) was chosen to carry the message to the enemy.
Here is his report:

> Appointed as a delegate of our fighting unit under the
> command of lieutenant 'Bloniak', I set out with the aim
> of reaching some understanding with the Krauts in the
> B.G.K. One leap and I was at the corner of Bracka Street
> and Jerozolimskie Avenue. Suddenly there were two shots
> from the Central Station, and I nearly got killed. I dis-
> regarded the firing and pressed on. At the moment of
> crossing from Bracka Street into Jerozolimskie Avenue I
> was in a blue funk, but my commandant yelled: 'Push
> on, Mickey, wave your white flag!' so I ran on. At the
> entrance to the B.G.K. I met three Krauts with their
> 'Sprayers' [machine guns] ready to fire. One of them
> cried: *"Komm mal hier!"* ["Come here"]. I approached
> and gave him the letter written by the captured pastor. A
> whole lot of Krauts arrived. They used to be so brave
> when they hauled people off the streets, but now they
> didn't look so confident. They asked where our com-
> mandant was and where our positions were. I said: *"Niks
> verstehen"* ["I don't understand"] and demanded an
> answer. The Kraut, furious, said: *"Keine Antwort!"* [No
> answer"]. I went back. I ran zigzagging, because I was
> afraid they'd shoot me in the back. I returned to the boys
> in our group and told them the whole story. We laughed

fit to burst. If all the Krauts are as brave as those here, Hitler won't get much joy out of them.

Thanks to Zenek's courage, a ceasefire lasting several hours was called the following day, so that the dead and wounded could be collected. In the evening, fighting broke out again. Pawel and Zenek took part in all their unit's sorties, and the insurgent press mentioned them several times in their bulletins*. And this is what appeared in the Insurgent Information Bulletin of 13th August 1944, in an article entitled: 'Antek the Sprayer':

> Antek-the-Sprayer and runner Nina were a well matched pair. He went to 'work', she cleaned the arms, loaded the magazines and carried ammunition. They were often accompanied by 13-year-old runner 'Mickey'. This tireless trio, always gay and energetic, was the apple of the eye of the whole detachment . . . Brought from the hospital on a stretcher to Antek's grave, the commandant, captain 'Sokol' bade farewell to his favourite in a short, soldierly speech . . . Little 'Mickey', brave Warsaw urchin, who had not been afraid to act as a negotiator with the Germans in B.G.K. (the National Economy Bank) cried like a baby. Today, Nina, Mickey and the rest of the group are still in the front line.

Towards the end of August the insurgents received the order to dynamite the German bunker at the corner of Bracka Street and Jerozolimskie Avenue. Pawel ('Urchin') volunteered to help the officers of the special task force. With a box of dynamite he crawled at night to the bunker. A sniper crawled behind him dragging an electric cable. A third man stood in the entrance to the courtyard of 12 Bracka unwinding the coil. As they finished placing the dynamite by the side of the bunker, two Germans entered arguing. Pawel returned to

---

* Article: 'Fighting Three' published in the information sheet A.K. *Fighting Warsaw* No. 31 of 13th August 1944. Article: 'The Youngest' published in the paper *From the Front Line* of 17th August, 1944.

his commandant and reported that all was ready. The lieutenant pressed an electric switch. There was a deafening explosion. Bunker and Germans blew up.

At the same time heavy fighting continued in the Old Town. The German ring tightened around the insurgents. Airborne squadrons circled the unprotected district, discharging their deadly load. Thousands were buried in houses which collapsed under bombs and shells. Hour by hour the Old Town was reduced to rubble. Stasiek-from-Praga was in the fighting unit of Captain Nalecza, where he was nicknamed 'Darky'. He was one of the bravest of the defenders, taking part in the battles for PASTA (the telephone service building in Tlomackie Street) and for the Polish Bank on Bielanska Street, where he was wounded in the leg.

Faced with a hopeless situation, the rebel command ordered the area to be abandoned, and set out to join the units fighting in the centre of town. Under cover of night the rebel units moved out, but they were hit by such murderous fire that they were forced to withdraw to their original positions. The following day it was decided to escape through the sewers. Unit after unit went underground, the rebel military police keeping order; even the wounded were brought down. The soldiers crawled one after another through the low, narrow canals full of filth, which resounded with the explosions of grenades thrown by Germans and collaborating Ukrainians. Some units headed for the centre of the town, the rest turned towards the suburb of Zoliborz.

After several hours Stasiek-from-Praga's unit reached the centre and emerged into the street. They were ordered to the barricade at the corner of Krucza Street and Jerozolimskie Avenue. There Stasiek met Pawel and Zenek, and a few hours later they found the Peasant and Chopper. The cigarette boys, overjoyed, celebrated till late at night. Before leaving for their posts, they decided to visit Granny on Krucza Street the following day.

Early next morning they organised some provisions, for they could not arrive at Granny's empty-handed, in spite of the famine in town. The boys reached no. 16 Krucza Street through holes in the cellars, tunnels and ditches, with a rucksack full of food. Granny's house had been partially destroyed by shells. One wing was occupied by an insurgent unit. The inhabitants crowded in the cellar made room for young armed soldiers. Pawel looked round.

"Where is Granny?" called Zenek.

"I'm here," answered the old woman from a corner. The boys pressed on through the crowd and handed her the full rucksack.

"My dear boys, you didn't forget me in my misery!" she wept with joy.

"We'll drop in again in two or three days' time. We won't let you starve," promised Zenek as they left. They returned to their posts.

The fighting continued. It became clearer and clearer that there was no possibility of the rebels taking over the whole of Warsaw. Their supply of food and arms decreased. Daily, huge losses in dead and wounded were inflicted on the rebels and the civil population. The German attacks grew in strength. In the middle of September the Germans gained a building housing the restaurant Cristal—an important point which dominated the surrounding district. Late that evening came the order to the rebels to win back the position, regardless of cost. A concentrated attack started at midnight, in which units from various districts took part. Stasiek-from-Praga, rifle in hand, was a runner in the front line. Pawel and Zenek handed on arms and ammunition. After a battle lasting nearly 30 hours the building was retaken by the insurgents.

Several positions changed hands many times, but the news that Praga had been taken by the Soviet and Polish Armies on September 14th raised the morale of the insurgents tremendously. Planes began to appear over Warsaw, dropping arms and food. Often the parachutes would be blown over to the German sector or into No Man's Land. Then, under cover of darkness, groups of insurgents—Darky, Urchin and Mickey among them—would have to creep in under German guns and retrieve the parachutes with their precious loads. The Polish Army actually sent some units over the Vistula, particularly to Powisle and Zoliborz, to help the rebels. But all this could not alter the over-all situation. The defended area shrank day by day. One post after another fell under the overwhelming enemy pressure. Because the Germans feared that the Russians would establish a bridgehead on the left bank of the Vistula, they used all their force in an effort to crush the revolt.

Finally after heavy fighting lasting 63 days, Warsaw capitulated. First Czerniakow, then Mokotow and Zoliborz. On the 2nd October came the turn of the Centre. According to the treaty of surrender the insurgents were to lay down their arms and give themselves up. The civilians were to be deported to Germany for forced labour.

Our cigarette boys found themselves in a difficult situation. They did not know what to do. The fear of discovery put them in especial danger. Zenek and Pawel turned to their immediate superior, Lieutenant 'Bloniak', and confessed that they were Jews.

"I think you should go with the army. If you leave with the civilians you may be recognised," he advised.

The boys decided to follow his advice. With their red and white armbands and the eagles on their caps they marched through the shattered streets of Warsaw into captivity. Endless columns of insurgents passed through the burning town. Beside them marched thousands of civilians; children, women, and old people, who went with no more than their misery on their backs. Among the civilians were Teresa and Halinka.

After a short stay in the temporary camp of Ozarow the insurgents were divided into groups and sent to Germany. Near Konskie one of these transports was attacked by partisans and several hundred insurgents, Stasiek-from-Praga among them, escaped to the woods.

Marysia and Stefcia found themselves with a group of 1,800 women insurgents who were deported to Stalag VIc. in Oberlangen. Zenek and Pawel were deported to the P.O.W. camp at Lamsdorf in Silesia. The living conditions and food were very bad. Several weeks later the camp was visited by a delegation of the International Red Cross; as a result all the insurgents received food parcels and English uniforms. A few days after this the camp authorities separated about 60 of the youngest prisoners and sent them to Stalag IVb. in Muhlberg, Saxony. This was an old camp with many thousands of prisoners of various nationalities. Among the multilingual and colourful crowd Zenek and Pawel met the Peasant and Chopper. Here conditions were not so bad, as they were supplied with food and clothes by the Red Cross.

A few weeks later all the young prisoners were sent to the camp in Brockwitz (Saxony) where they worked in various factories. In the evening the boys returned to the barracks and the real camp life began: they sang army songs, patched their torn clothes, furiously played card games. Often there were arguments and fights. The cigarette boys avoided getting mixed up in rows and never took part in fights; this, possibly, is what led to some suspicion being aroused among the Poles. They started a real hunt for the Jewish boys. The first victim was the Peasant, whom they tormented without mercy. After a while the Poles began to persecute Pawel and Zenek too. They could no longer walk through the barracks without being attacked. They were allotted a separate place to sleep and were pounced upon and tormented at every step.

Under the threat of denunciation to the Germans they were forced to clean shoes for their Polish colleagues. Their food parcels were confiscated. Sometimes one of the Poles would attempt to defend them, but then he too was attacked. The others were afraid to help the Jews. Finally the news of this persecution reached the nearby P.O.W. camp of officers from the 1939 campaign. One of them appeared in the juvenile camp and tried to explain to the boys the error of their ways, but without any effect.

The atmosphere deteriorated daily until the whole story reached the ears of the *Lagerfuhrer*. He summoned the Jewish boys, who, prepared for the worst, admitted the truth. But the German called up all the young prisoners and in a long speech demonstrated the injustice of their behaviour towards their comrades-in-arms. He threatened to use drastic measures if the persecution continued. It is difficult to judge what motivated his conduct—whether it was pity or the fast approaching frontline.

From that day on the persecution and insults, the confiscation of food parcels, ceased. But the Jewish boys still had to sleep apart from the others.

In the women's camp Marysia and Stefcia faced a similar situation. When these two were sent to Stalag VIc. in Oberlangen, they stood out immediately. In the camp they took part in a dramatic group. The two sang and danced well, but because of this they fell under suspicion and began to be tormented. Marysia and Stefcia were not cowed and proudly repulsed every attack, but the situation grew worse. But fortunately a group of Belgian prisoners in the nearby camp heard of their plight and threatened to take revenge if the girls were betrayed. This threat lessened a little the tension in the women's camp.

Meanwhile the front moved westwards. On January 17th, 1945, the Red Army conquered the Kielce district, where groups of Partisans were operating, among whom was Stasiek-from-Praga's unit. The following day the region of Grojec was liberated, which included Jasia. Immediately after the liberation of the capital, masses of the people of Warsaw returned to their city. Among the first to return were Halinka and Maisterek. Every day brought the liberation of more areas. The theatre of war moved to the very soil of Germany.

On April 12th the women's camp at Oberlangen was liberated, and Marysia and Stefcia stepped out to freedom.

As the Germans retreated from the attack of the Red Army, they reached the children's camp at Brockwitz, whence they took the prisoners to Meissen near Dresden. But on May 5th the Red Army entered these cities too. Pawel, Zenek, the Peasant, and Chopper returned to Warsaw. Some days later Teresa, who had been liberated in Berlin, also returned to Warsaw.

The cigarette sellers in Israel in 1970: left to right, Zenek, Pawel, and Bolus (back row): Amchu-man, Bull, Halinka, Joseph Ziemian, Conky, and Jurek (front row)

Epilogue

LIBERATION CAME and soon our young heroes found themselves faced with an unexpected problem: what to do with their magnificent freedom? They had no family or friends. They were alone in a crowd of happy, free people. In their long conversations they reconstructed the past. The future was more difficult to tackle. They were tormented by unspoken questions: Where to? What for? How?

But somehow they found the answers they needed. Today all those who survived are grown up. They have their own families. They have reconstructed their lives.

Who would have thought that this tall, handsome man— surely Israeli born, a 'Sabra'—wearing the uniform of an officer in the Israeli Army, was once little Bolus in a worn-out fur coat tied with string? And this enterprising business man from Niagara Falls, Canada: does he not look like Bull, the leader of the cigarette sellers from the Three Crosses Square? And still, in spite of his widespread business interests, Bull has not forgotten his old partners and keeps in touch with them.

Pawel drives a tractor in the Negev and his brother Zenek works in an Israeli arms factory. And who could have foretold in those days that three little Sabras would brighten Teresa's life?

162

Every morning, as the inhabitants of Israeli towns sleep the sleep of the just, Jurek brings the produce of his kibbutz to the Co-operative. His ten-year-old son would also like to be a driver.

Toothy has had his front teeth straightened, but the nickname has stuck to him for good. "I don't mind," he laughs. He is a highly respected furrier in Canada.

Conky works as a mechanic for EL-AL, the Israeli national airline and is the father of a growing family. The sisters Marysia and Stefcia, along with Jasia, Halinka, Kuba and little Stasiek are also all in Israel. The Peasant and Whitey fell in Israel. The others—Zbyszek, Baldy, Wladek, Carrot-top, Chopper, Stasiek-from-Praga and Fixer—remained in Poland or are scattered throughout the world.

Their friend the 'Amchu-man' is now a bus driver in Israel. He looks younger now than 20 years ago when the cigarette boys discovered him in his hole in the field. He dreams of taking all the ex-cigarette boys with their families on a special trip through Tel-Aviv.

The boys from the Three Crosses Square have not forgotten those who did not live to see the Liberation. They often remember the noble Polish boy Romek, and Hoppy and Frenchy who were not destined even to have graves of their own. They remember all those who helped them in those difficult times. And though they live far apart from each other, they are still now, as then, members of one big family.

Epilogue to this edition

ELEVEN YEARS have passed since this book was first published. And life goes on. Today the cigarette sellers are as old as their parents were at the time of the Holocaust. Their own children have grown up. Some of these children are now older than the cigarette sellers were during the period of time described in this book. Do the cigarette sellers now think about their past, reconstructing it for themselves and their children?

Perhaps not often. But they cannot forget, feeling as they must that the threat of Holocaust still hangs over their heads. Each new war in Israel brings the past back to them. Of course, many new problems have to be solved—problems connected with their present lives.

On January 30, 1971, the author of this book and the "patron" of the cigarette sellers, Joseph Ziemian, died after a short illness. Before he died, his friends visited him in the hospital, and he took leave of them as he would of the most treasured members of his family. The cigarette sellers have not forgotten him. They meet often in his house or at his grave to honor his memory.

As you know, the largest group of cigarette sellers settled in Israel; so, of course, they took an active part in the last two wars (1967 and 1973), fighting on all the frontiers. In the war of October, 1973, the only son of Jurek, Ejtan, fell while trying to pull his wounded commander out of the line of fire in a battle with the Syrians. The tradition of helping other people has passed from father to son.

Some of our heroes have changed their occupations since this book was first published; others have continued in their same professions, where they have been promoted and are earning good incomes. They have the energy and the will to succeed in most of their enterprises.

"Little" Bolus, as an engineer in an Israeli factory, has designed and built several new agricultural machines. He is the proud father of two young sons.

As a successful businessman in Canada, Bull can afford to visit Israel every few years to meet his old friends. Last year, he sent his 17-year-old son here for two months; next summer his 15-year-old daughter will probably follow in her brother's footsteps.

Pawel works as a commercial agent. His oldest son is in training as a pilot in the Israeli army; two other sons are still in school. His brother Zenek continues to work in a factory, advancing from time to time. His oldest son is finishing secondary school this year. His youngest son has not yet begun kindergarten.

Teresa was the first to marry; today she is the first grandparent in the group.

Jurek is working on a kibbutz, trying hard to find some solace after the death of his beloved son. He has two fine daughters. But who will carry on the family name, and who will say kaddish on his grave?

Toothy now lives in Canada. He has succeeded in his business as well as in his family life. He has visited Israel only once, but he married an Israeli woman, and they are the parents of three sons and a daughter.

Conky became one of the chief mechanics for El Al Israel Airlines. Because of his work, he often goes abroad. During visits to Canada or the United States, he never neglects to meet his friends there. This makes him a kind of ambassador between these friends and those living in Israel.

His oldest daughter is now serving in the Israeli army; the youngest child is only four years old.

In 1968, Halinka appeared in Israel. She could not bear the new wave of anti-semitism spreading through Poland after the Six-Day War. Today, she is working in a couture house. Elegant, sophisticated, smiling so prettily—she has changed from the girl who sold vodka and cigarettes near Three Crosses Square. But in her heart there is no change. Being alone, she takes an active interest in the lives of the other cigarette sellers. She also does everything possible to immortalize the memory of their former "patron."

Almost nine years have passed since the death of the Peasant, but the friendship between his two sons and his former friends has never been neglected.

Because all the other Israeli cigarette sellers live near Tel Aviv, it is not easy for Jasia to visit them often (her house is in the vicinity of Haifa), but she participates in all their reunions, the happy ones as well as the sad ones.

When Amchu-man died a year ago, all the Israeli cigarette sellers took part in his funeral.

Stasiek-from Praga owns a large grocery store in Philadelphia; Wladek became a businessman in Argentina. Fixer has a family in Australia, and Carrot-top is working in Brazil.

Others have ceased to keep in touch; life flows on, and some people change with time. But one thing has not changed. No matter where they are living and working, when the cigarette sellers meet, even after long periods of time, they still find themselves friends. What has united them cannot be erased from their memory.

Janina Ziemian
Holon, Israel
January, 1974